MW00576635

Jeff has done a marvelous job of reminding us what it means to truly love. *The Power of a Loving Man* will change your life and change your love.

—Stephen Arterburn, founder of New Life Ministries

The poignant account of a man's courageous trek toward vulnerability, authenticity, and love. Jeff's stories, that range from hilarious to profound, will impact your life forever in areas you have only dreamed of changing.

—Katie Brazelton, Ph.D., best-selling author of Pathway to Purpose™ series and licensed minister at Saddleback Church

Masculine love is the ten-megaton warhead that will take us from superficial to supernatural impact in the world today. Men everywhere will be thanking Jeff Jernigan for handing them the codes which unlock the real power to be God's man. This book is like the big, red button in our masculine journey, if we depress it nothing in our lives, as men, will ever be the same.

—Kenny Luck, pastor of men at Saddleback Church

When a man learns to love as he was designed to by God, the outcome becomes highly significant, in his relationships, his work, and his contributions to the world. Jeff has done a great job of presenting thoughtful and solid principles to help all men grow in this task.

—John Townsend, Ph.D., clinical psychologist, best-selling coauthor of *Boundaries* and author of *Who's Pushing Your Buttons?* He is also an international speaker and cohost on New Life Live Radio.

the power
of a loving man

the power

of a loving man

13 keys to setting your heart free

jeff jernigan

BROADMAN
& HOLMAN
PUBLISHERS

NASHVILLE, TENNESSEE

Ten-digit ISBN: 0-8054-4181-6
Thirteen-digit ISBN: 978-0-8054-4181-9

Published by Broadman & Holman Publishers
Nashville, Tennessee

Dewey Decimal Classification: 248.842
Subject Heading: MEN \ LOVE \ CHRISTIAN LIFE

Unless otherwise noted, all Scripture is taken from NKJV,
New King James Version, copyright © 1979, 1980, 1982, Thomas
Nelson, Inc., Publishers. Other version used include: RSV, Revised
Standard Version of the Bible, copyrighted 1946, 1952, © 1971,
1973; NASB, New American Standard Bible, © the Lockman
Foundation, 1960, 1962, 1963, 1968, 1971, 1972, 1973, 1975,
1977; used by permission; NIV, New International Version,
copyright © 1973, 1978, 1984 by International Bible Society;
and The Message, the New Testament in Contemporary English,
© 1993 by Eugene H. Peterson, published by NavPress,
Colorado Springs, Colo.

1 2 3 4 5 6 7 8 9 10   10 09 08 07 06

For Julia,
who loves courageously

Acknowledgments

I have come to realize that in my life I have often failed to grasp the power that was mine to set my heart free and to change the world in which I live through loving actions from a changed heart. That is the power of love as God envisions it and the apostle Paul describes it. I am not alone in this condition. As a child, student, military man; as a teacher, counselor, and coach; as a pastor, missionary, businessman, and human resources professional for nearly three decades, I have encountered many hearts in need of being set free. Those people inhabit the pages of this book.

Names have been changed and in some cases, stories have been combined to preserve anonymity. However, my story would be a poor lesson indeed without the testimony of these many men and women who have carved a future out of failure, discovering the power of love in the journey. For each one of them, all mentors unaware, I am indeed grateful. Thank you for showing the way.

A great deal of inspiration comes from Wally and Betty who, after more than sixty-five years of marriage, still find the humility to share the daily lessons they are learning in the

Lord about love that suffers long, is kind, and never fails. This heritage has been the fertile soil that my wife, Nancy, took root in, blossoming into an incredible example of love in motion. I see in you the best anyone could be. Thank you, Nancy, for opening the doors of my heart.

Thank you, Len Goss, for finding in these pages hope, power, and potential. Without your confidence and the superb work of the Broadman & Holman team, this message would never have seen the light of day. Your insight and counsel have helped make this book a true testimony to the power of love in a man's heart set free. Thank you as well, Kim Overcash, for your astute and timely insights as project editor. A good read is always a team effort, and for all the intentional and unintentional team members: Thanks for your part!

Contents

Foreword

Congratulations! You've just purchased a book that is much like picking up a "token" that allows you to cross a long suspension bridge. Here's why this token is so important to you. Imagine if there were a bridge you could cross that would take you from where you are today, to a place where you are more of the man Almighty God wants you to become. That's what I feel this book can do for you. By investing in the cost of this book, and the time it will take to read the short, helpful chapters, you're getting a token that can get you started on real life-change. In particular, instead of just guessing at what can make your own life and others richer and fuller, you'll actually "get the picture" of the power of a loving man. Why is that so important?

I'm convinced that men need pictures. For example, Jesus used pictures and stories constantly with his disciples. In laying down the picture of a biblical bridge—undergirded with God's Word and filled with head-nodding stories, Jeff Jernigan puts that token right in your hand. For you or your whole men's group, it's an invitation to cross a bridge that leads towards God's best.

Granted, sometimes picturing a bridge doesn't help. Like when I was speaking in the Oakland A's Stadium in Oakland, California, to over fifty thousand men at a Promise Keeper conference several years ago. I wanted so bad for the men of that city to "get the picture" of who they were, and even more, who they could be if they really understood and lived out God's love in their families. So I started my talk by using a picture that I felt sure would resinate with this huge crowd. Knowing that the vast majority lived in the San Francisco area where there were bridges galore, I started my message by saying . . . "Men! . . . Men! . . . Men! . . . Men! . . ." (Your voice echoes when you speak at a huge stadium.) "If you came across the Golden Gate Bridge this morning to get to the stadium, then I want you to stand up and let me hear a yell!"

I'm from Phoenix, Arizona, where the only bridges near me span empty riverbeds. But as I wrote out my message back home, an inspiration came to me. I could just picture hundreds of men who had crossed real bridges that morning, springing to their feet and shouting out that they'd crossed the bridge that day.

The best I could tell, out of the fifty-thousand-plus men in that stadium, five or six stood up and yelled that they'd crossed the Golden Gate bridge that morning. Slightly shaken, I tried another bridge.

"OK, if you crossed the Oakland Bridge to get to the stadium this morning, stand up and give a yell!" Probably a dozen more men stood up out of the many thousand present. It was probably the most embarrassing flop of an introduction I've ever given in any message, anywhere. My motives were good that morning, even if my knowledge of traffic flow patterns wasn't.

Those men needed to cross a bridge that day—to move from where they were to where they could be in loving God and loving their families. And you and I need to cross that bridge on this day as well. That's why I pictured a bridge to start my talk, and why I think "the biblical bridge" illustrated in this book really does work.

Men get moving when they can "picture" the target. As you head across the biblical bridge that Jeff Jernigan lays out for you in his writing, you'll find yourself picking up crucial knowledge and insights along the way. You'll finally understand what it's means—biblically—to be truly loving, and in the process, you'll come to see how incredibly powerful such a man really is for God.

It's my prayer that as this book makes its way through the hands of individual men and men's groups across the country (and I hope in the hands of many of these men's wife's hands as well), that I'll soon be able to say to thousands of them, "Did you come across a bridge today?" and the echoing cry will be deafening. Men just like you and me, who will lift up their voices to say, "Thank you Lord, for providing such a clear picture of what love really looks like in your Word. For understanding that real love is not puffed up or badly behaving, but is marked by bearing, believing, hoping and enduring all things."

So let me encourage you to start the journey. And in the process, see even more clearly the kind of love that will never fail you, or your family, because it's God's love flowing through you like never before.

—John Trent, Ph.D.

StrongFamilies.com

Introduction

Have you ever been loved exclusively? Has someone—your parents, spouse, friends, anyone—ever made you the uninterrupted focus of his or her attention, consistently had your best interests at heart, and guaranteed he or she would forever be selfless when it came to you? What would your world be like if you were loved this way?

My parents loved me totally when they were alive, and I know my wife's parents love me totally as well. My wife is in love with me, and I have a few friends I can honestly say love me in an appropriately manly way. But none of them love me exclusively.

Exclusive love is what God demonstrates toward us in a forever patient, kind way that is never resentful or irritated. Though I love others totally, I can never love them exclusively. At least not the way the apostle Paul described in his exquisite description in 1 Corinthians 13. Knowing that this is the manner in which God wants my love to be demonstrated toward others, even strangers, doesn't help me love more perfectly as a man.

At best there are moments when my commitment to others is devoid of self-interest, greed, pride, insecurity, and selfishness. But when those moments happen . . . Wow! The results are incredible! What would life be like if I could extend those moments and experience more of them?

Paul went on to illustrate how this kind of exclusive love works itself out in our relationships: In these moments we do not act out of self-protection, do not focus attention on ourselves, are not arrogant, do not act improperly toward others, do not strive to achieve something just for ourselves. Neither do we explode in temper tantrums, hold a grudge over the meanness or hateful acts of others, or secretly rejoice at the failure of others.

Exclusive love rejoices when those of us struggling with failure embrace the truth and accept responsibility. Exclusive love puts up with absolutely everything, continually has confidence in others, has only the highest expectations, and stands up under pressure to be less loving.

This is world-changing love, love that can never produce ruin for anyone, that can be counted on no matter what, and that never ever comes to an end! So why can't I love like this? What went wrong, and how can it be fixed? Why do I have such a hard time loving?

Perhaps I had poor parental models growing up. Or maybe it was childhood trauma that arrested my emotional development. Maybe it was the pervasive influence of society, dictating to me what it meant to be a man. Though these certainly are factors, the real problem—and the author of a limitation I cannot overcome alone—is my good friend Adam.

God needs no worship. He is infinite and complete—yet decided to share himself with us. Before the treachery in the garden, we were unaware of any incompleteness in ourselves.

Satan brought in discontent, and you know the rest of the story: we now feel the void and know the anguish of being estranged from God. Ever since then our behavior seeks to make complete the incomplete.

Incompleteness is not bad. It is part of God's design. It enables us to enter into appreciation for what God wants to share, equips us to find enjoyment in our relationships, and satisfies the deep needs of our souls. The struggle is over the autonomy we want in meeting those needs our way.

Adam exercised his right to choose in this regard. He chose not to convey to Eve his own understanding of God's expectations when he had the opportunity. He chose to abdicate leadership in the final moment when he could have intervened. Ultimately, he chose to participate in disobedience. Then Adam was afraid and hid, two new and precedent-setting experiences—not just for him but for me too.

Adam was not just afraid in the sense of worry over consequences of being caught. He experienced that devastating dread that hits the pit of our stomachs when we know we have really done something wrong. He experienced true moral guilt. He knew, and he felt fear.

In his now-imperfect world, what did Adam do when God came looking? He hid himself. What an interesting first reaction! Whatever changed in the garden at the moment deception was fulfilled in willful disobedience, its impact on the man was to create in him a flight response that is both physical and emotional. Certainly, a part of Adam's fear had to do with the mention of death in God's instructions in Genesis 2. However, the word used here includes the act of secreting one's self so that everything about you remains hidden.

Adam made excuses. He blamed the woman and even blamed God. Now, centuries later, we men still find ourselves making excuses, blaming others, avoiding responsibility for our problems; afraid of transparency and vulnerability, longing for intimacy and running from it at the same time because of the exposure risked. What used to be instinctive and natural is now a behavior that must be learned. No wonder Paul told the husband in Ephesians 5 that he must love his wife—it is no longer a given.

The reason I can't love exclusively is because I run and hide at the suggestion of intimacy; I fundamentally do not want to take responsibility for my problems; I am committed to avoiding pain and maximizing enjoyment; and I am only interested in you so far as you are able to satisfy my drive for safety, security, and significance. I would like to sugarcoat this reality and rationalize with you, minimizing this description of a man's heart at its worst moments. But the truth is there are times when I—we—are like this, and that is when I am most ashamed and the most in need of more work, golf, a good football game on TV, a distracting relationship . . . anyplace to hide.

In spite of these failures, Jesus loves me exclusively, dying for me even though I still fall way short of his expectations on a daily basis, and gives me the gift of change (Rom. 5:8). In Christ I am a brand-new person, continually changing for the better as a result of my relationship with him (2 Cor. 5:17). Men, it is possible for us to love the way God intended we should; and when we do, things like work, recreation, and relationships snap into their proper perspective, and the world changes.

My world has certainly changed! As you read this book, you will learn more about my pilgrimage as a man and about the miracles that occur in the lives of others—parents, children, spouses, friends, and colleagues—when men love exclusively.

All the tools, all the skills, all the secrets we need to succeed are locked up in five short verses in 1 Corinthians 13. Lived out, the message of this passage sets men free to love forever, forever changing the lives of those we touch.

Paul put love in perspective with his closing thoughts on the matter at the end of the chapter. Faith, hope, and love remain; but the greatest of these is love. Now faith and hope are both pretty big world-changing concepts. How can love be greater than these two? Perhaps one reason why this may be true is seen in how love emulates God. When we love the way God intended us to love, we see in each other something of who God really is; and in so doing, we glorify God.

Glory has tied up in it the idea of modeling or illustrating some truth about the object we worship. Loving others the way God designed us to demonstrates for them some truth about who God is, what he has done through his Son, and the response he desires but does not demand from us. Through love and loving behavior we reveal something of God to ourselves and to others, bringing glory to God. Faith and hope spring from our hearts, but only love can change the heart of a man. When men love from a changed heart, this small Christlikeness bursts upon their world with eternal consequences; and the world changes forever.

Chapter One

Love Suffers Long and Is Kind

Dan is special. The Lord took him when he was two and then gave him back. We were vacationing in Florida at the time. The adults were sitting in lawn chairs in the backyard and catching up on old times while the kids were down the grassy slope playing in the sand at the lake's edge. Over my shoulder I heard a voice clearly ask, "Where is Daniel?"

Since we always call him Danny, the question caught my attention. I looked around. No one was there. I looked down to the beach, and Dan was not in sight. I shouted to the other kids, asking where he was. They stopped playing and just looked around as well. My attention was drawn to a place just off shore; and I knew beyond a shadow of a doubt, just as if someone was standing there pointing, that Dan was there under the water.

I must have looked like a wild man charging down the beach leaping, swimming into the water. When I got to the place, I reached down; and his hair filled my hand. I pulled Dan out of the water and onto the shore. He was not breathing, his eyes were unresponsive, his lips and fingers blue, and there was no heartbeat. CPR did nothing to change his condition.

A passage of Scripture kept repeating itself in my mind: "In everything give thanks; for this is the will of God in Christ Jesus for you" (1 Thess. 5:18). If I had not been so panicked, it would have been annoying. In my mind I screamed at God, "I am NOT thankful!"

Then in tears I confessed that this child was his from the beginning and I was simply a poor steward of this precious life. If this was God's will, he could take him back, and I would be thankful. At that moment, with Dan's bare chest clutched to mine, I felt his heart begin to beat again.

All of the tests showed Dan to be healthy, none the worse for the near drowning. When he began to struggle in grade school just a few years later, we wondered if oxygen deprivation might have caused damage to his brain. He was a happy-go-lucky kid who would float from one thing to the next, never really able to concentrate long on anything. Simple things in school were difficult to grasp.

Dan didn't quite test out as learning disabled or experiencing attention deficit disorder. The results pointed to something, but no one could give us a definitive answer. The professionals pointed back to the accident as a possible cause. We held him back a year in junior high. We provided tutors from time to time. We tested and retested. Some teachers told us he was bright enough, just lazy; but I helped him with his homework and knew he was not lazy.

In fact, I went through the next seven years of school with Dan, fighting the homework battles, school projects, teacher conferences, and lost weekends. It was a long, excruciating haul; but we both graduated from high school. Those with challenged children know the hours it takes, the frustration for everyone involved, the self-recriminations, the endless stream of failures, the lingering questions, and the seemingly fruitless search for answers, or a reason, or relief.

Only God knows what, if anything, really happened to Dan that day. I can tell you now with great joy that Dan is a fine Christian young man, married, a decorated Marine veteran returned from Iraq, and successfully pursuing academic honors in college. When I think of the phrase "love suffers long," those years of helping Dan along the way come to mind. I love my son and do not regret for a moment those long nights invested in him. It wasn't suffering in the sense we understand that word these days. It was a patient, committed, accepting, and serving endurance—just like the apostle Paul talks about.

In 1 Corinthians 13, verses 4 through 8, Paul did a little bridge building, literally. This passage is constructed like a modern-day suspension bridge. The first pillar Paul created is a particular expression he used to name the subject, love—not just any kind of love but a unique and special love that is exclusive. He used a word for love normally attributed to God—something most assume is just not possible for us. Paul ended the passage with the same construction and grammar when he described this exclusive love as something that never fails. Suspended in between like a highway running from the first pillar to the last are examples of love worked out in daily life. "Love suffers long and is kind . . . love never fails" (vv. 4, 8a). When by faith we love like this, our world changes forever.

Dan's world is different. What would he be like if everyone had just given up on him? What would he be like if no one assumed responsibility and instead pushed it all on him? What would he be like if all he experienced in those years of struggle was criticism? My life is different too.

Now, nearly three decades later, I am beginning to understand that I was learning the discipline of patient kindness. Exclusive love is kind. Paul didn't mean here that we are simply to be nice to one another. This kindness looks out after the best interest of others and may not always be experienced by them as "nice." It is more than putting up with things in order to make things easy or better.

This kindness accepts others, admits weakness and failure, assumes responsibility, hangs in there, gives others the benefit of the doubt, and ultimately not only changes the object of such kindness but the giver of kindness as well. Tucked into Paul's choice of words is the concept that being kind has its own reward and somehow affects a change in me as well, whether or not it affects anyone else.

Many years ago I lived next door to a prostitute. When she began bringing her work home, I was furious. Often, since our apartment doors were next to each other, her clients would bang on my door looking for her. To make matters worse, this middle-aged lady had one leg. More than once she pulled up to the back of the first-floor apartment, and suffering from major intoxication and forgetting where she had left her leg, she crawled to my back door and hollered until I woke up, got her leg out of the car, and helped her to her own back door.

Yes, it was a kind thing to do. However, I was extraordinarily judgmental about the whole thing. Calls to the landlord did no good. Admonishing her clients did no good.

Berating her did no good. Nothing changed until I quit thinking about myself and started thinking about her.

So I apologized. I knocked on her door, and when she answered, I told her I needed to ask her forgiveness. I took the stunned pause as a sign I should hurry up with my confession before embarrassment took over and I chickened out. I asked her forgiveness for judging her, for working behind her back to get her evicted, for pretending to be nice when she needed my help when I really just wanted her to go away.

Eventually I heard her story. I found other ways to be genuinely helpful and patient with her struggling efforts—and failures—to be a different person. One day she asked the "why" question, and I told her about Jesus. Her life changed. She started going to church, found another line of work, and we ended up friends. Kindness has its own reward.

This is the same loving patience we experience in our relationship with Jesus Christ. God has carved out an exclusive place for us in his heart. From that place he constantly seeks our best interest and, in the words of the old King James Version, "is long-suffering to usward." This is tough for me. My image of fatherhood and manhood doesn't easily accommodate putting up with a lot.

My dad was a good man but stern, somewhat distant, a product of the depression. I knew he loved me because Mom told me so, and he acted that way. I am not sure I ever heard it from his lips, though. He died when I was eighteen so I never had the privilege of getting to know him as a person. He remains in my memory as a distant, busy, and not-too-involved figure. Unfortunately, that was my impression of what God was like and what my role as a father should be like as well.

When I act out of some sort of distant benevolence, it is impossible for others to feel that I love them exclusively, that the relationship is important to me, or because of that relationship and their contribution that I am different and better. That's what "suffers long and is kind" does to us. It makes us different and better.

Distance is safe for me as a man. God had to take me through some experiences to break down those stereotypes and change my world. If you believe God is not interested in you and does not want to be all that involved with you, you are dead wrong. There is an easy way to measure to what degree you may believe this. How distant are you from others who are really close to you? Would your parents, your spouse, your children, or your closest friends say there is an exclusive place carved out in your heart for them?

As we travel this imaginary highway across the suspension bridge the apostle Paul has laid out for us, we will discover more about how we can know God loves us and how others can experience our love without sacrificing one iota of our masculinity. Men talking about love is not an oxymoron. After all, God made us male, and it is good.

The metaphor of a suspension bridge focuses our attention on the journey. What happens to us along the way ends up being more important than getting to the other side. It is in struggling well—the working out of life solutions, the chance to see ourselves anew and to love ourselves well in the process—that profound change takes place. It means we have to redefine winning in terms of the experience and not the event.

Rock climbing has been a sport of choice in our family for more than two decades. Not the spandex-clad, monkey-like gymnastic nonsense you see in advertisements, where guys with zero body fat are hanging by two fingers without so much as a piton let alone a rope, grinning at the camera like there was nothing between their ears. No, we use harnesses, ropes, helmets, and some pretty mundane stuff to keep things safe while we climb. The grin on our dirty faces at the end of the day is from doing things well, not from doing them in spectacular fashion—and that is what I like about rock climbing.

It is not about getting to the top, or posing for some dramatic, death-defying camera shot to stick in your album, or conquering routes in record time, or putting up routes where no one has gone before, or looking manly while you strut around in the outdoors with all this gear hanging off you and clanking every step you take.

It is about learning to persevere and about learning to do things well. You see, climbing is about thinking through the challenge and coming up with a solution. It is about failure because not every solution is a success. It is about struggling well through fear, pain, and deprivation. It is about evaluating strategies, using techniques, understanding yourself and others, and putting it all together so that it works.

You may get to the top. You may do something unique, unusual, or noteworthy. But that is never the goal. The goal is to learn to do things well. It is all about the journey.

When I was still teaching rock climbing, this was the first and most difficult lesson to learn. Guys just like to win; and for most of the young men I was teaching, this meant zipping up the rock face like Tarzan and rappelling back down like Rambo. When this was not their experience, they felt like losers.

My first experience taught me to redefine winning. Some friends took me out, gave me some good basic instruction and a day of clambering over boulders to practice technique, and then tied me on the end of a rope and turned me loose. I was wearing a harness, and they were belaying me from above, so I felt pretty cocky. I watched two of them climb the face before it was my turn, and I was sure I could impress them with my skill.

After several embarrassing attempts to get started, scraping my chin and elbows, I finally flailed myself up the rock about twenty feet, found a big crack opening up in front of me, and threw my body in as far as it would go. This consisted of just my arm and shoulder and one foot. The rest of me was out there swinging in the wind. It wasn't pretty. What is worse, from my perch I could look out and down. The exposure panicked me. Twenty feet does not sound like much, but when you are exhausted, bleeding, and your heart is in the back of your throat beating your brains to death, everything takes on a different perspective.

They had to physically haul me up the rest of the way. I was in no shape emotionally to rappel down, so we walked down the back way. I was mortified. I felt like a total failure until, around the campfire that night, we talked about the day's activities and some of their first climbing stories. There was much I had to learn about the sport and myself before I would understand what winning in this endeavor—and life—really means. Until then, winning always meant coming out on top, winning the argument, doing better than the other guy, or just getting my way. I was always focused on the result or outcome I wanted and never paid much attention to the process.

Love that suffers long and is kind speaks of a patient endurance built over time and a kindness that results from a process, not just an act of kindness. It speaks of multiple attempts to learn and grow, to fail and succeed, and to redefine winning as more than just getting your way. As a man I am impatient with process. I want to master the skill now, accomplish the goal now, and achieve now!

Love is like rock climbing. It is learned best in the context of struggling well with what confronts you at this moment and then the next, and then the next, and so on.

I eventually got into good physical and emotional shape, mastered new skills (climbing is about technique, not strength), learned to manage fear and weakness, and became a halfway decent climber.

Not every climb in my career has topped out. Sometimes I wasn't up to the challenge, and sometimes I had to live with others in the party not being up to the challenge. However, I also have been privileged to climb in some of the most spectacular geography around the world with some fine people and enjoy every minute of it!

Paul laid out some challenges for us down the road. He asked us to consider things differently, do things differently than we ever have before. He asked us to engage in the journey, knowing that some days we will want to shout at the mountain and other days find a crack to crawl into. Know it is part of the process. Know that struggling well, not avoiding struggle, is the key to finishing well, to winning.

As a man I need to win now and then. It's in my genes and is part of what God made me. I don't ever want to lose sight of the goal but know now that winning—the outcome—will take care of itself if I pay attention to the journey. Like you, I just want a few good friends to accompany me along the way. I trust you will find them in this book.

Chapter Two

Key 1: Love Does Not Envy

Getting to a place in life where we can give and receive love that never fails is a process, and there are some practical things to overcome. Paul began with, "love does not envy." As we head down the highway, let's examine what it takes to love exclusively.

This is an interesting choice of words. *Envy*, sometimes translated as "jealousy," as used here represents a range of emotions from envious greed to fear of replacement. There is also the sense of intent. Whatever this feeling begins as, it ultimately results in action that, in this case, is inappropriate. Envy is not the problem. What envy becomes in real life may be.

Ron is an attorney I work with from time to time. The last time we were together, we spent the week in court on behalf of an employer. Each day we traveled back and forth to the courthouse in his brand-new, top-of-the-line, absolutely loaded, gorgeous BMW. I wanted that car or one like it. It spoke of prestige, power, and prosperity in a way any real man would find intoxicating. I am exaggerating, but you get the idea.

At some point I had to admit this is not the car for me. Impractical and way out of my price range, it was attractive to me for all the wrong reasons though they clearly were the right reasons for Ron. I gave up my envy as simply admiration for a fine automobile. To continue to desire to possess this vehicle— or worse, to go out and buy one—would have been allowing the feeling to result in inappropriate action. That is not love; it is lust. Lust controls us to the exclusion of love.

So guys, the next time a brand-new, shiny, four-by-four, quad cab, bed-lined, 380 horsepower truck sporting five coats of metal fleck paint zooms by you with a throaty roar, admire it; but don't obsess over it. It's OK to have the feeling. It is not OK to drool or let that feeling result in any kind of inappropriate behavior. What we set our hearts on ultimately will control us (Matt. 6:21).

This is challenging enough with material things. It can get really tough with people. When the object of our desire is a relationship, we move from envy to jealousy.

There was a time when my wife came to me to express a concern. A certain young lady, from her perspective, seemed to be paying too much of the wrong kind of attention to me. Now, at my age, that is flattering. Blasé on the outside, inside I was strutting. This is a dangerous attitude.

My wife does not want to be replaced in my heart by anyone or anything. This kind of jealousy can be good. God is called a jealous God (Exod. 34:14) because he does not want anything to replace him in our hearts. In fact, I don't want

THE POWER OF A LOVING MAN

anything or anyone to replace my wife in my own heart! I am
jealous of her place in my life.

I changed my schedule to eliminate unnecessary time
around this person, and we began praying that God would
turn her heart toward her husband. We prayed for our protection and theirs as well. The problem went away. But jealousy
can be an unhealthy emotion as well when it leads to the
wrong kind of behavior.

What if I acted on the stroking my ego got? Where would
that lead? What if my wife chose to respond defensively and
embarrassed everyone with an angry confrontation over
a perceived slight? The situation could have escalated into
something damaging to all the relationships involved. It is
a normal part of life to fear being replaced in someone's heart
or to desire a place in someone's heart that is just not there.
It is a different thing to act in self-interest to guarantee your
place.

That is the problem with envy in a nutshell. In one form
or another, it is an exquisite greed that acts out of self-interest
to obtain or control what it cannot possess legitimately.

Did you know the word for *envy* used here comes from the
same root as the word *zealous*? What are you zealous for? What
gives energy to your desires more quickly than anything else
does? What hole in your soul are you trying to fill?

When I was in training as a counselor, we had to analyze
ourselves in order to identify what some of our deep longings
were. These are the places we are most apt to take control away
from God, seeking to meet those needs—or protect them from
not being met—on our own terms. "On our own terms" means
someone else's best interests are not the focus of our efforts.
I cannot love exclusively if I am a greater champion for myself

than I am for you. Neither can I receive your love if I am busy pursuing my own agenda.

Greg is a friend of mine. In and out of counseling, he struggles with abuse heaped on him in the past, both physical and emotional. As a result Greg has come to believe he is worthless. Instead he believes his worth and acceptance are demonstrated and measured by the things he possesses. This includes a six-figure job, career awards, expensive cars, a fine home, a beautiful wife, and perfectly obedient children. In Greg's mind these demonstrate to the world that he is OK. Every ounce of strength Greg has is directed toward controlling this perfect world.

But, the world is not perfect. The job is falling apart, he has too much debt, the beautiful wife is fed up with his overbearing control, and the kids are rebelling. On top of that, Greg recognizes that the constant "wanting" never goes away, whether it is one more possession or one more idyllic relationship. Though his friends, his children, and his wife love him, Greg cannot receive their love because he fundamentally believes he is unlovable.

Men, to some degree, this is all of us. Control is a big deal for us, reflecting both the good and the bad outworking of our God-placed call to work and subdue the environment (Gen. 1:28). We need to make up our minds that we are going to do it his way, not our way, if we ever hope to get beyond envy and love exclusively. We were made to strive after the best in all things; and if we put the interests of others at the top of our list—and let Jesus focus on our interests—our striving will be free from envy and fear.

"For I know the thoughts that I think toward you, says the LORD, thoughts of peace and not of evil, to give you a future and a hope" (Jer. 29:11). God really does have our best interests at the top of his list.

One of the requirements for counselors in training was to do an internship under a bona fide, fully qualified and licensed therapist. This gave me a wonderful opportunity to peek into the lives of others, not just myself, and discuss observations with my mentor. Bradley was one of the cases we discussed progressively over a number of months. Bradley was a classic case of envy gone awry.

Bradley was a successful insurance salesman, married, with one son, Bradley Junior. Bradley Senior was envious of everyone with a bigger house, better car, higher-paying job, more prestigious title, lower golf score—you get the picture—and especially envious of dads with more successful kids. Bradley Junior played baseball, and that is what started unraveling Bradley Senior's world.

Fathers sometimes try to recapture missed opportunities or relive past failures with better outcomes through directing the experiences of their children. This effort for some sort of virtual exoneration and approval comes out of deep insecurities and turns otherwise good men into control freaks. The trigger for Bradley was envy.

Bradley also was the baseball coach for his son's team; and, by golly, his son was going to be the star, and his team was going to be the best in the league! So, when he was driving home late—delayed by the rain—from yet another road trip and called his wife to tell her to get Junior dressed and on the field in time for the game, he did not take it very well when he learned that Junior was sick. In fact, Junior had missed school that day because he woke up with a temperature and an upset stomach.

Bradley asked if the boy was OK now and learned further that his temperature was gone and he had a light lunch that did not seem to affect him negatively. "Well, get a uniform on the boy and take him to the game!" was the demand. In the argument that followed, Mom decided Junior was going nowhere. A cold, rainy night out late playing baseball was not what a sick child needed. Dad was furious and cited the following reasons:

1. If the coach's son doesn't show up, he (Dad) would be a laughing stock when they learned the boy was sick that morning but not that afternoon.

2. The pitcher they were playing against that night was easy to hit, and his son's batting average was just shy of the league record.

3. He (Dad) knew what was best for the boy, and he (Junior) needed to learn to buck up and take it like a man.

4. She (Mom) was the wife and needed to follow his orders! After all, she was a Christian, and it was her duty to submit to his leadership!

This last appeal for submission really frosted Mom. It's not that submission isn't a biblical concept—just that this was a very unbiblical and decidedly self-serving misapplication of the principle. In fact, when you lay out Bradley's reasons side by side, it becomes patently obvious that this was not about Junior at all. It wasn't even about Mom. It was all about Dad and his need to be in control and to look good.

This latest incident sparked another huge fight when Bradley finally got home, not just about the missed game but about everything else in their relationship that wasn't functional and had not been for years. When Bradley showed up for counseling, he and his wife were living apart. Her complaint was: "He never is satisfied! No one is ever good enough or smart enough. He always buys stuff we can't afford and don't need. He always wants and wants and wants, and no one can ever satisfy him!"

Men naturally want to possess and control. How we act on these God-given desires is what makes them constructive or destructive in our relationships. Love does not act out of self-interest to obtain or control what it cannot possess legitimately. When we do act this way, it always leads to the destruction of the very thing we seek.

Think of envy as an unhealthy greed. It may be for a possession like the BMW or that four-by-four, quad cab, bed-lined beauty. It may be a relationship. Bradley wanted a relationship with his son that he never had with his own father and perceived other dads on the team as having with their sons. It may be a condition such as having everything and more than your neighbors have because that is what you believe will make you secure, accepted, and respected. Wanting to improve our lot in life is actually a healthy drive. For Bradley, though, it was a matter of controlling the outcomes, making things happen more than trusting God for the outcomes.

Dealing with his envy, his unhealthy greed for things that defined his love for his wife and his son, became the door to understanding deeper needs for change. Slowly, as Bradley began to change, his wife and son began to change in response. The very things he could not force—their love, respect, admiration, trust, enjoyment of him—began to take shape in the relationship. Bradley Junior began to excel in school and in sports because he wanted to please his Dad out of genuine love, not fear. Bradley's world changed as he began to direct his energy toward controlling those things God has called us as men and dads to be concerned about while trusting him to meet the needs in our own lives left behind by the passage of time.

Love does not envy. This is the first thing Paul asked us to give up if we are truly to love. There was a deeper lesson in all of this for me. Bradley's counselor modeled patience and kindness throughout the process. Perhaps the kindest truth revealed in those interactions was the truth that none of us is perfect. We are all flawed to some degree, and most of us carry wounds in our souls no one knows about.

Parents are not perfect. Siblings are not perfect. Friends fail us. Teachers fail us. Our introduction to society and the process of assimilating our culture is fraught with pitfalls; and we often learn things the hard way, leaving scars and fears and hurts that haunt us later in life. Circumstances seldom conform to our expectations or even our needs, introducing us to disappointment and want. Most of the major choices are made for us early in life: where we live, go to school, and grow up—subjecting us to experiences we do not fully understand and certainly do not control. Our genetic makeup comes in part from mom and in part from dad, determining aspects of our looks and personalities. All of this affects who we are. Why, on earth then, with so much of this beyond our control, do we subject ourselves to the expectation of perfection?

We all start out as damaged goods with a choice. We can relentlessly pursue some unrealistic ideal and, when we don't achieve the ideal, we create massive facades to hide behind. Or, we can accept responsibility for what we can work on and let go of those things we must trust God for. Men like to look good and fake it when we know we are not. When Bradley learned he did not have to be perfect, that he was perfection in the making, it freed his soul. A life lived with Christ is the best classroom for learning to cope with what we are handed in life, good and bad. Graduation doesn't happen until we see him like he is face-to-face in heaven where we will finally be perfect.

This is not the last thing Paul asked us to consider giving up, but it is the first thing he asked for a reason. Loving as God intended men to love—their spouse, girlfriend, parents, children, siblings, colleagues, neighbors, anyone—requires we set aside self to some degree. This is courage in action—not just courage as act but courage as an attitude.

"Wait on the LORD; be of good courage, and He shall strengthen your heart; Wait, I say, on the LORD!" (Ps. 27:14). David knew—as a shepherd exposed to the wilds, a soldier preparing for battle, a king in need of wisdom, and a man faced with choices in life and love—that courage ultimately comes from the Lord. He is the strengthener of men's hearts; and as we wait on the Lord, we will be sufficient for what lies ahead.

Chapter Three

Key 2: Love Does Not Parade Itself

Paris in June, there is nothing better! However, we were sitting there in abject embarrassment. The foursome next to us had practiced a thinly veiled conceit for the better part of an hour, humiliating us, shaming themselves, and fully acting the part of the ugly American.

Business gave Nancy and me the opportunity to travel regularly throughout Europe. I spoke French, she spoke Spanish, and we managed to get along quite well in most places. Over time we had adapted the dress, attitudes, and some of the mannerisms of our hosts. In other words, we did not look like or act like Americans. Certainly we were not experts at passing ourselves off as something else, and that had never been our motivation. We were interested in fitting in, acknowledging the privilege of being a guest in someone else's home country.

In Paris we did not pass as French; but our French was good enough, along with our attitude and appearance, to convince most that we came from somewhere on the Continent. That and business contacts allowed us to develop many acquaintances and friends over time. One of those friends owned a restaurant in downtown Paris in the heart of the tourist district not far from the Eiffel Tower.

We were sitting at our table just inside the open café area that spread across the entire front of the restaurant and opened on the shop- and apartment-lined street. It was as picturesque a setting as you would ever dream of, and we were looking forward to a long, comfortable evening of quiet conversation and fine dining.

The foursome had swaggered in, loud and bold, sometime earlier. It was evident one of the couples was living in Paris. He was an American businessman, and she was his American wife. The other couple were her parents. They were visiting the kids, and the son-in-law was clearly very proud. He was also loud, impatient, rude, insensitive, and egotistical.

Overhearing the three of us, I am sure he assumed we were natives. What's more, as the conversation progressed, it was clear he believed we could neither speak nor understand English. Our amusement at this situation quickly turned to chagrin as this young man began to tell his folks how awful the French were. His wife was no help, heaping her criticism upon his; and Mom and Dad joined right in. The manner in which they treated the waiters was right out of a bad movie. Some of their arrogance was even directed toward us. When they began bragging about America and the way we do things so much better, I wanted to cork his mouth with the bottle on their table.

Through all of this, our friend the owner and his staff treated them like visiting royalty and did not respond once in an unkind or inappropriate manner. Nancy reminded me that even in America they may act this same way—some people are just idiots and no single culture has the corner on that market. As we discussed our neighboring expatriates further, something else became clear. They were totally unaware of how they were being perceived. In fact, as we sat there observing, it occurred to me that with a different setting, say Chicago, or Raleigh, or Seattle, or San Diego, I probably would not notice them. They would seem quite unremarkable, even unnoticeable.

So why was I so offended? Was it because I had become so accustomed to my host culture? Was I somehow more culturally sensitive? I don't think so. What I think is that I was looking into a mirror. There were plenty of times in the past I am sure I had been the ugly American, culturally unaware and insensitive, ethnocentric as it were. We were in such a unique situation that the differences were amplified, exaggerated in a sense beyond what we would normally experience or notice.

Everyone in some small way believes that he or she lives in the best times, in the best place, among the best people, and has the best answers. The world revolves around us, and we are the yardstick by which everything is measured. This is true for small children and, in some ways, adults never get entirely past this youthful conception. What this foursome was demonstrating— and what I was demonstrating in reverse—was our conceit.

Conceit in its most constructive form is an idea or concept, something conceived or imagined in our mind. In its most destructive form, conceit is an unwarranted inflation of our own vanity rooted in a fear that we just don't measure up.

Love has a foundation not in conceit but in Christlikeness. The apostle Peter summed it up very well:

> Grace and peace be multiplied to you in the knowledge of God and of Jesus our Lord, as His divine power has given to us all things that pertain to life and godliness, through the knowledge of Him who called us by glory and virtue, by which have been given to us exceedingly great and precious promises, that through these you may be partakers of the divine nature. . . . But also for this very reason . . . add to your faith virtue, to virtue knowledge, to knowledge self-control, to self-control perseverance, to perseverance godliness, to godliness brotherly kindness, and to brotherly kindness love.
> (2 Pet. 1:2–7)

Obviously, parading yourself around is not a loving thing to do. Love is not conceited and does not parade itself. Paul suggested this kind of self-love must be overcome if we are to love others exclusively without self-interest.

Makes sense—we guys can strut around like a bunch of roosters cockle-doodle-doing our achievements like a collection of merit badges. A little bragging never hurt anyone; and if I don't toot my own horn, who will? However, this kind of conceit is more than getting all puffed up, vaunting ourselves over others in some kind of testosterone-driven competitive spirit.

The word Paul chose to use here, and the way it is used, goes deeper than that. This conceit is rooted in a mental attitude that says deep down we have set up our own personal judgment as the standard of truth—what we think is true simply because we think it is true. My opinion is right, and I am not going to change it because, at some level, I believe I may be wrong; and I cannot afford to be wrong. I am the standard.

Cliff grew up under the shadow of a talented older brother in a successful family. He didn't choose the best of friends to hang around. Somewhere along the line he decided to set up his own thoughts and feelings as his yardstick for making any decision. Insecure and suspecting his own inadequacies, Cliff became his own standard of truth. There was a great deal of safety there, in a place where truth was relative and he didn't have to defend himself since no one could challenge him with a greater truth than that of his own opinion.

Years went by. Cliff even forgot how he ended up being so opinionated and, much to the amusement of his friends, would rather avoid discussing controversial issues because he knew already what his opinion in the matter was—he just could not remember how he got there. Well, you can imagine how someone with really strong opinions who refuses to discuss them comes off in a crowd. Cliff didn't have too many close friends as an adult.

Eventually, his world fell apart. Unable to escape the snare of this self-protective love, communication at home broke down and rumors of affairs abounded. Eventually Cliff wound up out of work, divorced, alienated from his children, and deep in debt. His world could have been so different if he had been able to let go of some of those opinions, beginning with "be right at all costs."

Roger did change his world. Roger was one of those guys who always looked just a little too good, had all the answers, and left everyone in the dust when it came to achievements. His conceit grew beyond embellishing details, stretching the truth, or exaggerating a story. Roger crossed the line into fraud and ended up getting sued for his misrepresentations. He lost his job, his reputation, and his credibility, and embarrassed his family and friends in a very public way.

Unlike Cliff, Roger chose not to stick to his guns. He took a long, hard look at himself and accepted responsibility, made restitution, and started on the long road to recovery. It took a traumatic—and humiliating—event to get through. Roger had to accept that God does not make junk and that his value is not determined by his peers, his parents, his world, and especially not by his opinion.

Nowadays Roger enjoys the prestige of an important, well-paid job he came by honestly and the rewards of restored reputation and credibility. The new freedom he feels to be transparent and vulnerable in relationships has drawn him into greater intimacy with his wife and children and changed their world forever.

Cliff and Roger are real people, but they could just as well be metaphors for you and me. There are times when I have been committed to my opinions out of pride, embellished a story or two, and been a little too full of myself. Underneath it all I recognize the fear: *Have I got what it takes? Am I as good as these guys? Will people like me? Am I important? Do I count?* When I strive to answer these questions for myself in a way that puts up the best front for others to see, I am really acting out of self-interest that is greater than my interest in others. My conceit diminishes my ability to love.

When Nancy and I were getting to know each other casually, she would always ask me for boyfriend advice. After a while I stopped giving advice. I really liked this girl. If we were to ever get together down the road, I didn't want to be found guilty of feathering my own nest at her expense. This was frustrating for her and our friends since my job in effect was counseling—giving advice.

I wasn't always this secure (and occasionally am still not), but this is not the greatest risk I took with the woman who would eventually be my wife. When the time came, I chose to get us involved in premarital counseling. Nancy had never been married before—I had—and we both had a lot of serious questions and doubts about moving forward. The greatest risk was when I asked the therapist who treated my first wife and me to do the premarital counseling.

This Christian psychologist was not only my counselor; he was part of my accountability group and had been given releases to talk to a number of individuals connected to me at church and at work. This guy knew more about me than I did, including how selfish and manipulative I could be. I asked him to tear us up, leave no stone unturned, no secrets hidden. He did. Ouch!

Fundamentally, I understood that without a change in my own self-appraisal I was almost guaranteed to repeat the past and that many of my failures found their origin in my conceits. What a blessing to discover unconditional love in the heart of a woman who remains to this day the finest person I know. My world has been forever changed. By choosing not to parade myself around emotionally, I not only opened the door to loving others more selflessly; I opened the door to receiving love.

God has such a vested interest in us and values our friendship so much that we don't need artificially to inflate our worth for the world to see. "I have loved you with an everlasting love . . . though those dearest to you may forsake you, I will take care of you . . . you are precious in my sight, and I will give people for your life" (paraphrase based on Jer. 31:3; Ps. 27:10; Isa. 43:4).

It is difficult for men to know when we are parading ourselves. There is naturally a little bit of the rooster in each of us that works against being self-aware in this respect. For me a number of self-checks have proven helpful. When in a group of guys that I don't know, how soon do I go to the, "What do you do for a living?" question? Too easily we can measure ourselves professionally against others. *Where do I fit in? How do I rate?* These are parading questions we ask ourselves almost unconsciously. When guys are telling stories about one thing or another, how quickly do I jump in and tell my own story (that is, usually one-up on the story just told)? Our natural bent to compete can kick in at just the wrong times.

Conversations about what I own, what I do for a living, and radical experiences I may have had expose me as a member of the parade. The facts are not wrong in themselves. Sharing these things at this time and in this way reveals my true motivation. Most often when I am at a gathering of some sort with men involved, we rarely talk about where we blew it, our most recent embarrassing failure. What we talk about are our successes: our big deal, our latest acquisition, our triumph at work, how we magnificently handled a situation, where we won. Again, it is not that we shouldn't talk about these things. It is all about why we are talking about these things and what it reveals about our purpose. We want to be known as strong, competent winners.

Listen to yourself sometime. Is the conversation you are a part of all about you? In other words, as you converse, is the dialogue about you in some respect—your family, your job, your interests, your experiences? This is parading.

I attend a lot of formal business functions as a routine part of my business or in support of my wife's business. Consequently, I get to meet many new people. I try to ini-tiate conversation around an inquiry about the other person. It never ceases to surprise me how easily some people can go on and on about themselves. In part this is because so few people show genuine interest in us. In part, it is because we like parades.

At one of my wife's company events in which I was the "husband of Mrs. Jernigan," I took this tack with the husband of the host. He was prolific in his descriptions of everything related to his career, his patents, his accomplishments, his . . . just fill in the blank. I nodded, grunted a time or two, asked a few clarifying questions, and that was it. We never got around to me. In fact, I wasn't even sure he knew who I was.

On the way home my wife mentioned to me that I had received a compliment. Naturally, I inquired as to the nature of the compliment, all the while my chest swelling rooster-like. Evidently, this fellow to whom I had been listening said to his wife and mine that I was the most stimulating and brilliant conversationalist he had met in quite some time. Go figure. I was there for his parade, and that is all that mattered.

There is a proverb that helps me keep things in perspective. "Let another man praise you, and not your own mouth; A stranger, and not your own lips" (Prov. 27:2). I wish I could tell you I am not convicted by this as often as I am. But then again, sometimes I am a rooster. My goal is to let others invite me to their parade far more often than I may be inviting them to mine.

Guy is a friend of mine. I have known him for less than two years; and I think we could be best friends, given enough time. He certainly is the kind of person I respect and admire. Guy is the husband of one of the ladies my wife knows through her volunteer work. In fact, their relationship occasioned our introduction.

Guy is pretty laid back, not a fancy dresser in casual settings, and shows a real interest in others. He doesn't talk much about himself. Yet at the same time Guy knows how to be appropriately transparent and vulnerable, not wearing his emotions on his sleeve but coming across as real and genuine. I liked him immediately.

Eventually, I learned that he is an attorney and has thick skin when it comes to jokes about sharks, bottom feeders, and all that other abuse heaped on the profession. That was about it.

Now let me tell you what else I have learned about the guy, and not so much from his own lips. Guy owns one of the most successful law firms in his particular discipline. He also owns a restaurant and a lot of expensive real estate. He is even a landlord for some of his properties.

Guy has been behind some of the most successful ministries in this country, is legendary in his generosity, and gives more that isn't tax deductible than is acknowledged with receipts. Active in missions, he wants the backseat support position and views his role as making others successful, not himself. Knowing more now about Guy's background, you would never predict such extraordinary success from such humble beginnings. Among a group, however, he is just one of the guys. He has no parade, except the one I give him here. Guy will be the first to tell you he is not perfect and be honest about what that means. Guy doesn't hide behind false humility; and I marvel at how readily he fits in, accepted by others as "one of others" without pretension.

No one facing Guy professionally in court or outside the courtroom in more informal circumstances would ever mistake him for anything less than a man's man—a lesson to me that favor with others, reputation, and admiration are not obtained through love that parades itself. My world is certainly different for having known Guy.

Chapter Four

Key 3: Is Not Puffed Up

A rrogance is a good word to describe what being puffed up is all about. Paul linked it grammatically back to "parading" oneself around as an illustration of what happens to us when we take ourselves too seriously. When we begin to act as if we are better than others—know more, do more, and know it and do it better—we are guilty of arrogance. If you have ever been around arrogant people, you understand what a major turnoff this can be.

Nebuchadnezzar was arguably the most powerful ruler of the ancient world. His father, Naboplassar, threw off the Assyrian yoke when he destroyed Nineveh. Nebuchadnezzar married the daughter of Cyaxares in a political move to unite the Median and Babylonian dynasties. This was the beginning of the end for Assyria and Egypt as world rulers.

Nebuchadnezzar had the finest education and training that Babylon could provide. He was raised believing his time was the greatest and that he was the greatest among the greatest people on the earth.

With an alliance with the Medians solidified, Dad sent Neb to oppose the Egyptians who were occupying western Syria and Palestine as part of their alliance with the Assyrians. The Assyrians had lost their capital city when Nineveh fell and had moved the seat of government to Haran. Dad chased them out of Haran as well, forcing the Assyrians to set up headquarters in Carchemish, and that is where he sent his son to face off with the Egyptians.

Carchemish turned out to be one of history's most important battles. Evidence suggests the city had been around for some three thousand years before Christ and served as a major trade intersection sitting on an important crossing of the Euphrates. Control of this city meant control of nations.

Nebuchadnezzar arranged for King Josiah from Israel to move Jewish forces into Pharaoh's path at Megiddo as a delaying action. Josiah was killed in the battle (2 Chron. 35:23–24). Necho's army was delayed again at Riblah (2 Kings 23:33), so that when he finally arrived at Carchemish, Nebuchadnezzar had already captured the city fortress. Nebuchadnezzar then soundly defeated the Egyptians, ending the Assyrian Empire and reducing Egypt to a second-rate power. Babylon was now the undisputed ruler of western Asia.

Nebuchadnezzar returned to Babylon upon learning of the death of his father. You can imagine the welcome this brilliant world-class military strategist and victorious warrior received when he came through the gates. He then undertook the remodeling and expansion of Babylon, creating the greatest city in the ancient world.

The Old Testament book of Daniel tells us much about Nebuchadnezzar's perspective on life at this point. He had also become the world's most arrogant man.

Nebuchadnezzar had a dream in which he saw a huge statue made of various metals, beginning with gold and descending to iron mixed with clay. Daniel interpreted the dream, telling him that the gold head was the Babylonian kingdom that would be replaced in time by other less powerful kingdoms.

Later Nebuchadnezzar forgot this lesson and had an entire statue made of pure gold, stating that Babylon would last forever, and required people to worship the image. This is where the three men in the fiery furnace come in, reminding Nebuchadnezzar again that what God says stands and that God alone is supreme—not Babylon.

He still didn't get it.

> All this came upon King Nebuchadnezzar. At the end of the twelve months he was walking about the royal palace of Babylon. The king spoke, saying, "Is not this great Babylon, that I have built for a royal dwelling by my mighty power and for the honor of my majesty?" While the word was still in the king's mouth, a voice fell from heaven: "King Nebuchadnezzar, to you it is spoken: the kingdom has departed from you! And they shall drive you from men, and your dwelling shall be with the beasts of the field. They shall make you eat grass like oxen; and seven times shall pass over you, until you know that the Most High rules in the kingdom of men, and gives it to whomever He chooses." That very hour the word was fulfilled concerning Nebuchadnezzar; he was driven from men and ate grass like oxen; his body was wet with the dew of heaven till his hair had grown like eagles' feathers and his nails like birds' claws.
> (Dan. 4:28–33)

Well, that put an end to Nebuchadnezzar's parading. The rest of his reign was significantly different, and he died quietly at the age of eighty-three. To this day most of the bricks archaeologists dig up in Iraq have his stamp on them. Nebuchadnezzar underwent a real change of heart:

> And at the end of the time I, Nebuchadnezzar,
> lifted my eyes to heaven, and my understanding
> returned to me; and I blessed the Most High and praised
> and honored Him who lives forever: For His dominion is
> an everlasting dominion, And His kingdom is from gen-
> eration to generation. All the inhabitants of the earth are
> reputed as nothing; He does according to His will in the
> army of heaven And among the inhabitants of the earth.
> No one can restrain His hand Or say to Him, "What
> have You done?" (Dan. 4:34–35)

Even the most arrogant among us can reform. Yet the world often sends us a different message.

From what the media tells us, it seems like being puffed up is just part of being a man. In fact, this often is the excuse: it is not really arrogance; it is just part of the male ego. Certainly some of what we may see in others and read as a little chest-bulging may be part of our masculinity, but that does not go far enough to explain or excuse why some guys are just over the top with their "just us guys" behavior.

True masculinity develops out of personal, social, and cultural contexts. In that sense there is no typical male behavior. Our masculinity is learned in the context of our family structures, our social interactions at all ages, and our ethnicity. Masculinity, as it were, is an adaptation to social and cultural demands we face every day.

Though similar themes may exist among groups of men, each man finds his own identity in different ways than other men simply because we do not grow up in the same families, have the same childhood experiences, attend the same schools, or come from the same parts of the world. We face some of the same demands as other men but also face very different demands as individuals. Bottom line: We cannot blame aberrant behaviors on our gender. The kind of arrogance that results from being puffed up goes way beyond the traits of behaving in ways considered typical for men.

Another convenient excuse we hide behind is the Testosterone Myth. "It's the hormones! I've just got too much testosterone!" Testosterone has a larger-than-life reputation. Testosterone is involved with the growth of muscle mass and strength, increased bone density, height growth, formation of the scrotum and development of the male sex organs, deepening of the voice, and the appearance of face and body hair.

However, it is the connection to arrogance and aggression that has contributed to the stereotypes of "boys will be boys," "raging hormones," "sex fiends," and other masculine clichés. Testosterone has been thought a primary cause of aggression in males, making it easy to blame everything from puffed-up parading to violent aggression on too much testosterone.

Actually, testosterone is a hormone both males and females have. It plays a role in the well-being of us all. What's more, it is not the cause of aggression. Sure, testosterone is linked to aggression; but when scientists began asking the question, "Which came first, the chicken or the egg?" they came up with an astonishing answer.

Aggression elevates testosterone. Testosterone, in turn, fuels assertive behaviors. That tells me it's all in the mind. The place where control of our assertive, cocky, puffed-up, parading attitudes begins is in the mind. The apostle Paul said in

Romans 12:2 that the way to avoid being conformed to the world's way of thinking is to be transformed in the mind.

In my generation masculinity is defined very much by what you do alone and with other men. I participated in athletics in high school and college, playing competitive soccer through age forty-three and competitive tennis through age fifty-three. I have spent many wonderful days in the wilderness hiking, hunting, and fishing with friends or just by myself. I have driven motorcycles and flown airplanes. My wife and I are still avid rock climbers and skiing enthusiasts, and enjoy both more in the company of others.

All of these have elements of learning, doing things well, challenge, competition, and winning tied up in them. It could just as easily have been a list of work-related things rather than recreational activities: getting promoted, succeeding at work, closing the contract, or making the deal. This element of struggle is a natural part of masculinity just as it is a natural part of life.

What was not listed was getting lost in golf, softball, bowling or any other adult sports league. Becoming a couch potato during any given sports season was not on the list. Getting lost in an endless progression of home improvement projects or becoming a workaholic where the job is concerned wasn't on the list either.

Now none of this is bad in moderation. I watch the Super Bowl, and I even follow a few teams in a variety of sports throughout the year. But I don't memorize all the players' names, their vital statistics, or what product they recommend for jock itch. I cannot tell you what all the team logos are or who set what record last, or any of the vital team statistics that guys seem to argue about endlessly when they have nothing else to talk about—the problem. Most of us get buried in these things because we are hiding; and we toss it off as just being one of the guys, a man, and part of our masculinity.

Well, it's not. It is typical avoidant behavior, and the question becomes: What are we avoiding? For Adam it was exposure of inadequacy, something intimacy almost always guarantees will happen. If we are to love others as God loves them, it means getting close. Getting close is another term for intimacy. Getting close means risking exposure; people may get close enough to see us as we really are. So we throw up the fortress walls and cover them with a façade of masculine bravado that, when carried too far, becomes arrogance.

Most of us do not carry things that far. We just go on hiding. One of my favorite hiding places used to be work. I was hiding behind my masculinity as the provider, breadwinner, and solver of all problems great and small; when in reality I was avoiding pain. Logically, you might say at this point that my coping behavior just continued the pain, adding more fuel to fire. From my perspective the pain of avoidance was less than the pain of confrontation. Isn't that just like us men, choosing the lesser pain?

If the truth were known, I would love to have figured out how to make the problem go away. I just didn't have an understanding of how to do that. I didn't have the words to say or the skills to use, and I did not want to ask because I believed it would make me appear weak and unmanly. Help came in the form of an older Christian friend and mentor who eventually helped me understand, gain the words, and develop the skills needed to separate and deal with my issues.

Guys, the manly thing to do is to get help—a friend, a mentor, or a counselor—and learn what you may be hiding from and how to deal with it. In the long run it really is more masculine and a lot less painful.

Biblical masculinity for Jesus and for us is pictured in Isaiah 32:2: "A man will be as a hiding place from the wind, And a cover from the tempest, As rivers of water in a dry place, As the shadow of a great rock in a weary land." Someone puffed up with arrogant pride cannot love exclusively, but this kind of man can. This kind of man is courageous, strong, wise, enduring, and masculine. Coworkers, neighbors, friends, family, and loved ones, when they encounter this kind of person, see a little piece of Jesus and are drawn to him, not repelled by him.

Love is not puffed up. What will it take for us to see where we have become puffed up on a regular basis? Well, for me it was a set of problems I had no answers for that became severe enough that I went looking for help. I would not recommend that approach.

Do you know someone who has the respect of peers in terms of the qualities described in Isaiah 32:2? Take some time and ask him what he thinks it means to be a man. Compare those answers with your own study of what it means to be a hiding place, a cover, rivers of water, and a shadow of a great rock.

The better you understand your masculinity, the less likely you are to hide behind it. Find ways to spend more time with people, especially those with some degree of personal connection to you, doing more than yackety-yacking about this week's big game. Find a mentor or counselor who can help you discover your motivations and build new skills.

Be confident that your identity is ultimately in Christ who loved you enough to become the ultimate hiding place. "But God demonstrates His own love toward us, in that while we were still sinners, Christ died for us" (Rom. 5:8). Hiding in Jesus is a good thing.

Moses is another world-class leader who chose to forego the arrogance of his youth for a more humble approach to those he loved. Moses was the adopted son of Pharaoh, who preceded Pharaoh Necho. Moses had all the same privileges of Nebuchadnezzar: growing up in the home of a world empire ruler, treated with deference and enjoying luxury beyond measure, trained in military and political art and science as a future ruler. The Old Testament book of Exodus gives us some good illustrations of his arrogance, including one that resulted in the murder of a countryman. That final act of arrogance sent him into the desert for forty years in exile. However before that happened, Moses was a pretty powerful guy, and he was puffed up over it all.

Moses's sojourn in the desert, assuming the role of a shepherd, getting married, and raising a family shaved off some of his arrogant corners and let some of the air out of his puffed-full sails over the next forty years. Taking on the responsibility of leading the children of Israel out of captivity and to the promised land further refined his character. So much so, that we read of him, "So the LORD spoke to Moses face to face, as a man speaks to his friend" (Exod. 33:11). Now that's something! To be called a friend of God—there is nothing puffed up about that.

God reserved that opinion for few people. Enoch walked with God (Gen. 5:22–24) as friends do. Noah, called a just man, walked with God in this same way (Gen. 6:9). Abraham was called righteous long before the Old Testament law defined what righteousness was because he believed God when God spoke to him about life in the fast lane and what would come tomorrow. God promised Joshua, Moses' understudy, that he would be with him in the same way he was with Moses (Josh. 1:5). King David summed up why it is so hard to be puffed up when God is your friend. "You will show me the path of life; In Your presence is fullness of joy; At Your right hand are pleasures forevermore" (Ps. 16:11).

Moses had a lot of conversations with God, beginning at the burning bush where God called Moses into service. These included instructions before meeting Pharaoh given over a number of conversations, numerous conversations about the plagues, and important information about the Passover. There were also conversations about the Ten Commandments and then that awesome confrontation when they were handed over. Rules and regulations were worked out in a running dialogue. At Mount Sinai, God initiated a series of conversations about what lay ahead that continued for years, and then there were those disciplinary reproofs when the children of Israel just couldn't get it right. By the time the tabernacle was built, providing a means for an imperfect nation-in-the-making to relate to a holy God (again, built based upon instructions from God), Moses had plenty of face-to-face time with God.

The antidote for being puffed up is clearly found in an intimate, personal relationship with God incarnate, Jesus Christ. If you are having the kind of regular conversations with Jesus that Moses experienced, there will be little room in your life for arrogance. When Jesus makes us his friend and we respond as only a friend can, the arrogance just melts away.

Chapter Five

Key 4: Does Not Behave Rudely

The speaker had just finished the presentation, and a number of us were standing around talking to the event organizers. Walking up to the group, another one of the event leaders suddenly butted into the conversation and loudly berated everyone in hearing about a number of problems with the event.

How rude, I thought! What in the world was he thinking? To criticize the leaders for their organizational skills in front of a number of participants was unbecoming behavior, and it was not in keeping with the values we had just heard espoused from the podium.

How did this person arrive at this moment so full of venom? What compromises had he made emotionally that left him so bereft of situational awareness? This matter of compromise is an important one because it sneaks up on guys often. It is easier to see the connection between compromise and unbecoming behavior when we illustrate the problem on a larger scale where the consequences are more than just embarrassment or hurt feelings.

In business the importance of compromise to getting things done is clear whether it is a business decision that must balance competing interests or a career-advancing personal issue. These kinds of compromises are commonly called trade-offs, compromising one good thing for another good thing. There are also compromises that require trading off something good for something bad.

A compromise between food and poison, for example, is obviously a poor trade-off. The poison wins every time. However, most compromises of something good for something bad are never this serious or carry such transparent, destructive consequences. Yet this is exactly what we do—usually because the poison is unidentified or the potential negative consequence so slight that it seems acceptable in light of what may be gained by the compromise.

Enough bad compromise over time may accelerate your life into an early crisis. Here are two true-to-life situations in which the opportunity for a bad compromise is obvious.

As executive vice president, your job is to review management meeting notes and produce the minutes that usually contain action items for participants to follow up on and report progress on at the next meeting. Customarily, you give the president a draft of the minutes to review before disseminating a final copy to everyone.

Almost every time you review the draft with the president, he instructs you to change something. It might be a date, a dollar figure, a comment someone contributed, or some aspect of a consensus opinion or decision.

Only one problem, the changes reflect things that didn't happen or that weren't said quite the way the president wants it to appear in the minutes. After a while a pattern emerges. The president is manipulating the minutes to move his own agenda ahead. You know he has a reputation for getting rid of people who don't cooperate. What are you going to do?

Here is another scenario. The boss where you work has a tendency to force out people he views as poor performers or those he simply does not like. In most instances this has been handled well, and the employees really did need to move on. In some cases, however, employees have been terminated without cause under a manufactured and factually untrue set of reasons.

The company is downsizing in the face of a declining market for its product. The boss instructs you to include a number of employees in the planned layoff who have done nothing wrong, are actually good performers, and would not normally be included in the layoff because of the crucial nature of their positions or their seniority in the company. When this is pointed out to the boss, you are instructed to make something up—just get rid of them.

Standing up to the boss when asked to do something unwise or possibly unethical from a business perspective rather than placate the boss's ego is the only thing these employees may have erred in. If you don't find some magical way to include them in the layoff, you will be guilty of the same resistance. What are you going to do?

Both of these examples ended in a poor compromise. What's more, these small decisions—made poorly—led to other poor decisions, each with a weight and direction to them that eventually led to the end of a stellar career for these executives.

What went wrong? What began as occasional "less than the best" choices can easily start us down the road to failure, even jail time. How can we avoid this pathway? What are the signs to recognize before we pass the point of no return? Learning to recognize the poor decision before it is made and the compromise it constitutes is crucial to staying out of trouble altogether.

There are three conditions that set us up for compromise at an almost unconscious level: lack of awareness, underestimation of our own susceptibility, and little understanding of the process of compromise. Men are decision-makers. We live in a world of constant change in business realities as well as the social context in which business is carried out. Every opportunity we are faced with to conduct ourselves poorly is actually an ethical conflict. In a fast-paced environment, being unaware or unprepared to deal with ethical conflicts makes it easier to go with the flow than if we were aware of the implications of our choices.

The individual butting into the conversation at the beginning of this chapter would have been better off if he had taken a moment to pause, reflect on what he was about to say, and then choose the right moment and the right words to communicate his feelings. Also, the executives who lost their jobs would have been well served by this practice of pause, reflect, and choose. There is real wisdom in the proverb, "Keep your heart with all diligence, For out of it spring the issues of life" (Prov. 4:23). Eventually, what is in our heart becomes reflected in our behavior, "For as he thinks in his heart, so is he" (Prov. 23:7).

We tend to think highly of ourselves, and in a world where opportunities to make a poor compromise occur without warning and, therefore, can slip by without having been subjected to thought, we can also think of ourselves as not at risk. When this risk is not recognized, we tend to view compromise as an unlikely event, something that will not happen to us. With a sense of invulnerability, we end up making bad choices by default simply because we were not mentally or spiritually prepared.

If we lack a group of friends who can positively influence our moral compass, we become isolated from any kind of helpful check and balance to our heart. Without any unethical intent, bad compromise begins passively to occur. Peers, friends, and coworkers see it, but we don't; our frames of reference do not allow it. It becomes very easy to justify and rationalize behaviors in which we may not normally approve.

Living in a world that requires some sort of compromise on a daily basis is like slowly cooking on the stove. Something happens to change us over time, too slowly to notice as it is happening but obvious over time that a difference is being made. Let's say you put three pots of water on the stove to simmer. In one you put carrots, in another you put eggs, and in the third you put coffee.

After thirty minutes you return. The carrots that went in stiff and hard are now soft and pliable. The eggs that went in fluid and flexible on the inside are now hard-boiled, more rigid and less flexible. In each case the water has not changed, but the carrots and the eggs have changed dramatically. On the other hand, the water in the pot with the coffee in it has changed dramatically. It now has taken on the flavor and aroma of coffee.

Whether the pressure to compromise is personal (originating within you) or external (a function of your circumstances), it can change you. With enough poor choices you may become soft and pliable like the carrot, doing what everyone else is doing. You may become more like the egg, reacting with resistance to the pressure to conform; but being hard-boiled, you may find yourself ostracized simply because you have become too inflexible. Most of us would choose to be coffee, affecting the environment around us, a model of good choices. I have had my share of carrot and egg kinds of compromises.

During my separation I made some bad decisions. I chose to get involved with questionable relationships. I put myself in places and situations that left me open to criticism. I confided in untrustworthy people. I included some people in my accountability group out of political correctness and not because they had something to contribute. I exposed myself unnecessarily to speculation, rumor, and innuendo.

I responded to judgmental attitudes with anger and judgment of my own. This only fueled what was going on. It certainly was not loving.

People confronted me at my place of work and berated me in front of coworkers. Others called clients and encouraged them not to do business with me. Some even demanded my employer fire me. I had to obtain restraining orders—which really helped my popularity! My children became alienated in the process, something still not entirely healed today. Financial debt grew considerably, a hole it took nearly a decade to climb out of. I lost a lot of friends; and my world became a moonscape, airless and cratered.

You might say I acted rudely. Again Paul chose his expressions carefully so that they stand alone as a concept and at the same time point to a conclusion, an "aha!" down the road. Here the idea is that unbecoming behavior is a function of volitional choice, not accidental coincidence, moreover, that the truth of the matter will be obvious. Paul is right. My choices were not accidental. They had a purpose.

It reminds me of conversations I would have often with my friend Bill while we shared counseling notes. Bill was a licensed psychologist, and we shared offices in the building where he had his practice. Bill would always say after describing someone's behavior, "All behavior has purpose!" That purpose may be inconsequential most of the time but not all of the time. A person's behaviors will give you insight into their purpose and personality. So what was my purpose?

I was looking for salve for a wounded heart, but I was looking on my own terms, in ways that I could control. The Bible has something to say about this: "For my people have committed two evils: They have forsaken Me, the fountain of living waters, And hewn for themselves cisterns—broken cisterns that can hold no water" (Jer. 2:13). Each little decision I made looking for comfort, acceptance, or approval had a small weight and direction to them that ultimately determined the outcome. I should have been looking to Jesus, using His strategies and not my own. "Come to Me, all you who labor and are heavy laden, and I will give you rest" (Matt. 11:28); "God is our refuge and strength, A very present help in trouble" (Ps. 46:1).

What Paul was saying here, without having to spell it out, is that love is a choice and that choice is driven by purpose. If that purpose is selfish or self-protective, it is not love the way God intended and we will act improperly. Men, we must be careful with our little choices, understanding that they act like a compass pointing to our purpose. Sometimes we just need to stop and ask ourselves: *What in the world are we doing? Why would I do this on purpose?*

Try to make a habit of making even the little decisions well, not just the big ones, especially if there is a relational dimension to the circumstance. Nowhere was the importance of this pointed out to me more than in a layoff experienced by a friend.

The owner brought his son in to run the company. The son hired competent professionals to build the business to new heights of success. My friend was fortunate enough to be part of that stellar team. Once the company had gained momentum, the owner decided he would take a more active role. Unfortunately, he drove the business with a style that created no end to negative politics, backbiting, jealousy, and strife. Eventually, the son left in frustration.

Instead of allowing himself to be drawn into the fray, my friend made sure every day that things were done decently and in order, that people were treated with dignity and respect. It often put him at odds with the owner. Soon the stellar team was gone: quit, terminated, or outplaced. It was my friend's job to handle those transactions. It was very tempting to just lay low, do what everyone wanted, and be co-opted one small decision at a time into a lifestyle of intrigue and compromise. He treated the boss and his new team with the same dignity and respect he had enjoyed with his previous colleagues.

Three weeks before he was to be let go, word reached him through a loyal friend. When the day finally came, my friend made sure his office was empty and everything on his to-do list had been done and done well. "It is just not working out," was how the conversation started. From the body language it seemed as if there was an expectation my friend would explode in a temper tantrum—not the first time this had happened. Instead, my friend simply stated that he understood, shook his hand, and processed out with a generous severance in hand.

It doesn't seem like much. But now, so many years later, I still hear news of lawsuits going back and forth with so much acrimony. His little choices along the way have protected my friend from such things, and his world is so much better and different than it could have been—all because he chose not to act rudely.

The same kind of attention to small things characterizes my relationship with Nancy. I call her during the day, every day that I can, to see how she is doing. After all these years I still ask her out on dates. I communicate regularly how much I enjoy helping out around the house or just running errands with her. I listen when she talks. I let her read my mail, go through my pockets and get stuff out of my briefcase because I am committed to an open relationship. The fact that she treats all of this with gratitude and respect makes it even easier.

Small things, all of them, but they have made my world a much more wonderful place than it was so long ago. These kinds of choices have restored my integrity and my reputation and given me a new understanding of living by biblical principle.

Tell me, friend, what direction is your compass pointing today? Here are some things that will help guard you from acting rudely in your relationships with others.

1. Be prepared to make ethical choices. Don't ignore or forget the opportunity to pause, reflect, and choose.

2. Develop for yourself a few values that you practice regularly. For me these are very simple and very basic.

a. My word is my bond. Because this is true, I don't give my word lightly. I have been "the boss" a number of times in my career. In each case this value created more relational capital and trust than anything else. Employees that knew I would keep my word even to the point of personal sacrifice were the most loyal even through adverse circumstances.

b. Always get the third story before making up your mind. There are always at least three sides to a story: yours, theirs, and what really happened. Before making a decision, going after what really happened, instead of just my experience or opinion has saved a lot of heartache over the years.

    c. Seek out creative alternatives. The first good idea may not be the best idea. Other good ideas may be better. When confronted with a bad compromise, appeal to alternatives that will accomplish the same thing in a more appropriate manner.

You will have other values that work for you, that anchor your behavioral choices when it comes to compromise in what is good and right. The point is to make sure you have them and use them.

    3. Don't isolate yourself from peers, family, friends, and other social contacts that can help you maintain equilibrium. Avoid developing patterns that wed you to your work. Patterns lead to habits, and bad habits lead to bad conduct. Habitually practice widening your perspective on issues by disallowing your world to shrink to the size of your office. Ensure there is a healthy spiritual dimension to your life.

    4. Don't be in a hurry to make a decision. Few things are life-and-death decisions that need acting upon right now. Haste and convenience are the enemies of healthy compromise. Take your time. If it doesn't seem right, think it through.

    5. Make sure your moral compass is grounded in biblical principle and not what is commonly accepted as appropriate behavior. What the world accepts is sometimes less than what God expects of us.

These tips don't hold the promise of keeping you from making mistakes. People bent on being bad will, well . . . be bad. Others simply need to be aware of how bad things can get if they don't pay attention, especially to the little things. Understanding we are at risk and taking steps to heighten our awareness and minimize the risk will keep most of our mistakes in the arena of the faux pas—something easily recovered from. Here is a checklist that may help you identify areas of compromise.

1. Do you ever pad expense reports?
2. When you hear of someone else's good fortune or promotion, do you silently criticize them in your thinking?
3. Do you hold grudges?
4. Do you exaggerate on your résumé?
5. Do you fudge on your tax returns?
6. When someone compliments you on a job well done and you know the credit should be shared, do you correct him or her and share the accolade?
7. In your reports to your boss, do you downplay the negative and accentuate the positive, or do you give both fair treatment?
8. When you tell stories, do you only include your successes, or are you equally transparent about your failures?
9. Do you skip out on a restaurant meal without leaving a tip?
10. Do you speak poorly of people when they are not around?

If you answered any of these in the affirmative, you have admitted to a bad compromise. The question remains whether or not these things are an accidental or incidental occurrence in your life or a habit that needs to change. Love that does not act rudely begins where small compromises are avoided.

Chapter Six

———◆———

Key 5: Does Not Seek Its Own, Part I

We can love many things: our country, job, family, friends, a girlfriend, a spouse. In seeking the best in these circumstances and relationships, we are encouraged not to strive for an outcome that is solely for ourselves. Love is not ambitious for self. Now, *ambition* is a big word. It encompasses a range of things from good to bad and in between.

In Christian circles the idea of ambition is often understood negatively. So we are going to spend some time looking at this idea of being ambitious for self. It's not all bad news. We need to step back for a moment and look at male ambition from a larger, less personal perspective in order to separate what may be biblically motivated and what may not. Let's start with the job.

Ambition as a career perspective is much misunderstood. For many, the word *ambition* conjures up images of arrogant, self-seeking personalities willing to do anything to get ahead. For others ambition is some sort of secret chemistry, the absence of which is a sign of laziness. Ambition is not a pejorative. In its simplest form, ambition is the desire to achieve, the motivation and willingness to pursue a goal or an aim.

My gifts and training equip me to make a difference. In fact, I am happiest in my work when I know I am contributing. You might say my goal is to make a positive difference in the situations in which I find myself every day.

The opposite of ambition is complacency—not a bad thing either if the situation calls for some degree of contentment or satisfaction. The Latin word *ambitio* was used of political candidates in Rome making the rounds soliciting support for their goals. In this case it was to be elected. It is easy to understand how the word came to be associated with a desire for fame, power, and wealth in some not-so-positive ways while the lack of ambition became somewhat synonymous with underachievers. However, the link we want to focus on is the connection between desire and achievement. Ambition is crucial to achieving any important goal. Our goals need to be larger than something we simply want for ourselves.

David, a famous—or infamous—character in the Old Testament (depending on how you look at it), was ambitious. Sometimes it got him in trouble. Most of the time he was ambitious for God and for the benefit of others.

His boyhood began humbly enough, living the life of a shepherd. David was clearly gifted with many talents and, as he grew, became known for his musical talent and later for his conspicuous valor. Eventually he was anointed as King Saul's successor.

Before he could ascend to the throne, still years in his future, Saul forced David to live as a fugitive and outlaw. David never raised his hand against the incumbent king and even spared his life. Throughout these years are stories of David's heart for others and of incredible things accomplished on their behalf, even though, as the anointed king-to-be he didn't have to do anything at all.

Saul's death resulted in a political crisis for Israel, and civil war followed. David eventually became king, and the war between the house of Saul and the house of David ended with the virtual extermination of the house of Saul. David went on to become Israel's greatest king. He also made some tragic mistakes along the way, consequences of which followed David the rest of his life. In spite of this, history records for us a great compliment:

> And Samuel said to Saul, "You have done foolishly. You have not kept the commandment of the LORD your God, which He commanded you. For now the LORD would have established your kingdom over Israel forever. But now your kingdom shall not continue. The LORD has sought for Himself a man after His own heart, and the LORD has commanded him to be commander over His people, because you have not kept what the LORD commanded you." (1 Sam. 13:13–14)

David is called a man after God's own heart. He was more ambitious for God than he was for himself.

The Christian man who pleases God acts out of an ambition that trusts God and not himself for power and strength to achieve. Like David, we want to please God, trust his Word, and long to be free from the tyranny of our own selfishness (Ps. 19:7–14). David's ambition for the Lord and for others led to many great things. Though his life was far from perfect, it demonstrated that even an imperfect life is capable of love that does not seek its own.

It is important that we not misconstrue ambition. There is an ambition that is unhealthy. "Let nothing be done through selfish ambition or conceit" (Phil. 2:3). There is also an ambition that pleases God. "But it is good to be zealous in a good thing always" (Gal. 4:18).

I once consulted with an organization that viewed ambition as a character flaw. As a fundamental element of the corporate culture, it did not matter if ambition was a positive influence inspiring vision and commitment or a negative reflection of more personal goals. Any kind of ambition was perceived to be spiritual immaturity.

This perspective can take root more easily in purpose-driven organizations than others. Everything must be sacrificed for the vision, aim, or mission. We move forward toward the goal together; success is recognized as a group result. Purpose-driven leaders in this environment are hailed as torch bearers, even heroes. The group shares in the limelight created by a leader in pursuit of the corporate calling, as it were. If the leader gets out too far in front of the followers, however, he or she can quickly become a martyr. It no longer appears to be about the mission or the group but about the individual.

As the individual succeeds, the group no longer shares in the success in the same way. Fears about the group's goals emerge. Differences of opinion, especially about how to get things done, accentuate. Eventually, the amount of change required of the followers to continue down the road taken by the leader is too great, and the relationship breaks down.

This same organization I just mentioned was faced with a rapidly shrinking market share, burgeoning operating costs, and a crippling lack of customer focus. It engaged consultants, created focus groups, benchmarked other organizations, and eventually decided some major organizational change was needed.

An internal task force was created, drawing from the company's talent pool from all over the world. The group spent three years assessing, designing, and building support for large-scale organizational change.

In tackling some of the systemic challenges behind the larger problems, this task force had the opportunity to work with different business units within the organization. In experimenting with out-of-the-box solutions, they created a new sense of freedom and, in producing credible solutions, developed a following. Eventually a strategy emerged that everyone including top management and the board bought into.

Then came the fish-or-cut-bait day. Everything went fine until three things were required:

1. Outplacement of individuals in the field determined to be in a poor fit with the requirements of the new directions.
2. Decentralization of control and authority.
3. A change in leadership at the national level.

As the change process began to bog down in the face of passive-aggressive resistance, the task force members, with the support of various business units, stepped in to address the obstacles. These were men and women drawn from the organization's leadership cadre in the first place. Already acknowledged as positional leaders, they also bore the new mantel of successful leaders in the new endeavors. It became clear that top management, at one time in support of the changes recommended, were digging in their heels when it came to any decisions affecting them personally. They were seeking their own, so to speak.

When pressure to follow through with earlier commitments began to emerge from the field, the "ambition card" was played. Top management insinuated that these emerging leaders (i.e., the task force members holding them account-able to the plan) were not the right ones to lead the charge. Their ambition was for themselves and not the cause. In this particular culture, that was a message swallowed hook, line, and sinker by the rank and file. Influencing change became harder and harder for this group until it became impossible. Some task force members left the organization in frustration, some tried to force the issue and were asked to leave, some went off the deep end and rebelled, and a few went quietly back to old jobs. Over a period of six months, they were all gone; and change was a dead issue.

Tragically, the organization was left somewhat of a mutant: not what it used to be but certainly not transformed into what it could have been either. Some of the best talent left, and nearly two decades later they have not recovered their for-mer organizational prowess. It is really too bad because every-one on that task force was ambitious for the cause and never for themselves. Certainly, there were task force members with genuine character flaws, but ambition was never the problem.

The irony of the whole process was in the ambition that was displayed not by the task force members but by those most threatened by the change. Rather than be ambivalent about ambition, we need to treat it as essential and slightly danger-ous, at least when it is poorly motivated. Bottom line: the right kind of ambition on the part of individuals and groups is behind every lasting positive achievement. "He who waits on his master will be honored" (Prov. 27:18). "Whatever you do, do it heartily, as to the Lord and not to men" (Col. 3:23).

Ambitious people, in the right sense of the word, are optimists, believing in the eventual reality of success. They persevere toward the goal, demonstrating an endurance char-acteristic of a high degree of motivation. In many respects this means I must tame my own ambition lest it lead me into compromise and failure. Never allow success or the potential for success to intimidate you. By the same token, never allow success to go to your head. When you do, you enter into the world of self-seduction and start down a path that ends with your being convinced of your invincibility—a very dangerous ambition. Selfishness, greed, poor compromise, and clinging to power corrupt good ambition.

This was so clear to me in Moscow. We were there to produce a historic conference for the general of the Russian Army. Over six hundred top generals convened for a week to learn from a Western perspective how to deal with the challenges of a downsizing military in a bankrupt economy. Everything from dealing with suicide and alcoholism in the ranks to turning engineering battalions into construction companies was discussed. There was also the opportunity for the patriarch of the Russian Orthodox Church to address the assembled military regarding reintroducing Christian chaplains into the army.

My buddy Bruce had roped me into serving as the program director for this event. Bruce was the president for Olive Branch International, and this was the first major international event for this fledgling organization. In a special audience with the patriarch, Bruce and I received the blessing of the church and were commissioned to reintroduce Christian values to the Russian military.

As you can imagine, this was a big deal. Newsies, politicos, and wannabes came out of the woodwork on both sides of the Atlantic, wanting to make this their moment in the sun. We got to see firsthand how selfishness, greed, poor compromise, and clinging to power can corrupt good ambition. In the end selfless ambition won out.

The patriarch got his opportunity to address the generals; and because of the sacrifices of many wonderful donors, volunteers, teachers, pastors, and organizations, the conference was a success. Olive Branch has grown and gone on to serve around the world, making a positive difference for the gospel in hundreds of thousands of lives. For these people the world has forever changed—all because a few did not seek their own.

Not seeking your own always begins on a deeply personal level. Dean and Jessica are well into their eighties. Dean and I go to the same church and often share a cup of coffee together and just talk about life. When Dean's wife of more than a half century had a hip replacement complicated by arthritis and then soon after lost much of her sight, Dean's world caved in. They could no longer take long walks together, go swimming, play golf, or play cards with their friends. Dancing was out of the question, and other complications put most travel out of reach as well.

Jessica, after some understandable and difficult adjustments, bounced back just fine. She found a way to play some card games, take short walks, go shopping with friends, and change their travel plans to accommodate the new situation. Dean took longer to bounce back. He found himself now in the role of chief cook and bottle washer. Add to that housecleaning, errand running, grocery shopping. Dean also became Jessica's eyes to the world, reading books and newspapers out loud, describing the movies they still watched together, reading the mail, writing her letters, and all of the tens of thousands of little things we take for granted when we can do them for ourselves.

At first he resented the intrusion on his freedom. Dean was angry and discouraged with this sudden change in fortunes and then felt guilty when he would lose his temper and snap at his sweetheart. To do these things for Jessica, Dean gave up a lot of what he used to do. True to his character, though, Dean was honest with himself and God about his selfishness, and slowly I watched his ambition transform into a new dimension of love for Jessica that did not seek its own.

I have always had the greatest respect for Dean and really held him up in my mind as an example. I would have had zero criticism and only praise for his relationship with Jessica before all this happened. Over the months we talked about these things, I watched a man transformed by the insights he was gaining about what being truly selfless requires. What I also saw was how a commitment to loving in a way that does not seek its own not only changes the world of the object of that love but changes even more profoundly the world of the lover. If you ask Dean, he will tell you he has gained far more than he lost. If you ask his friends, they will tell you their world is better, different, changed just for having been there to watch it happen.

There are times when we do seek our own quite purposefully, and, like Dean, we catch ourselves remorsefully wishing we could replay the moment differently. Give yourselves a break, men—it happens to all of us. Like David, we are not perfect; and, like David, we can still accomplish great things in that imperfection. The emphasis Paul used in the phrase "does not seek its own" focuses on the incessant seeking, searching, and striving to achieve something for yourself in the relationship. Selflessness is the exception rather than selfishness. Paul was saying, "Hey, let it go! Build a pattern in your life of focusing on others, and things will take care of themselves."

There is room for failure. In fact, if you think about it, failure was Dean's readiness learning moment. He never would have gone deeper if he had not been confronted by his own shortcomings, and he chose to make those shortcomings the exception and not the rule in his relationship with Jessica. David and Dean, however, don't even begin to illustrate what not seeking your own is all about.

Chapter Seven

Key 5: Does Not Seek Its Own, Part II

As an executive coach and counselor, I have had the opportunity to work with many people I would consider great when it comes to selfless ambition. This has been true in my experience as an employee in the workforce as well as a marine. You probably would not recognize any of their names. What made their ambition qualitatively different? I believe it was a willingness to put the interests of others ahead of their own in the spirit of Philippians 2:3–4: "Let nothing be done through selfish ambition or conceit, but in lowliness of mind let each esteem others better than himself. Let each of you look out not only for his own interests, but also for the interests of others."

Isn't it interesting that in this thought of Paul's there is a linking of ambition and humility? This is true as well in 1 Corinthians 13:4–8, but that is an insight for the next chapter. Suffice it to say at this point that there is a link between ambition and humility when it comes to love as a man—two words we would normally understand to be worlds apart. Selfless ambition is not possible without humility.

These great leaders I mentioned had something in common that helped define their ambition. They all had a passion for authenticity, a passion for excellence, a passion for making a difference, and a passion for spirituality in the workplace. These women and men endured and persevered. They insisted on adding value to whatever endeavor they were involved in. They were fun to work for and be around. Most importantly, they were committed to empowering others and saw success as the outcome of "we" efforts and not "my" efforts.

Here are a few questions to help you check your ambition:

1. Do you inwardly cringe when someone takes credit for something you accomplished or materially contributed to?
2. Do you join those recognized for their accomplishments, rejoicing and celebrating with them, or do you secretly resent their success and fear being overshadowed or left behind?
3. When you are recognized, do you share the credit?
4. Do you enjoy going to work every day?
5. Is there a sense of moral obligation to the quality of decisions you make?
6. Do these questions make you uncomfortable, preferring to be less vulnerable or transparent even with yourself?
7. Do you acknowledge the accomplishments of your peers and subordinates?
8. If you were to list the things that really energize you, would the list include what the organization you work for has as its mission or goals?

9. Are you really interested in contributing to the improvement of work life where you are?

10. Are you really interested in improving the human condition as an outcome of the product or service you or your company provides?

I must say, I cannot answer all of these in the affirmative. I trust that most of the time my conduct and decision-making reflect some degree of compassion and altruism—at least enough that I am not caught honking at my own taillights trying to get ahead. The fundamental question is one of focus. Whose successes are you focused on most of the time?

Moses knew early on that he was not going to make it into the promised land. That meant someone else with the right mix of leadership, spiritual maturity, and experience was going to have to fulfill his ambition. Joshua became the focus of his preparations for the future of Israel.

When Joshua was chosen to be Moses' successor, he already was a great leader (Exod. 17:9). Already the head of one of the tribes (Num. 1:10), Joshua was a proven general in battle (Exod. 17:8–13). That is like asking the leader of a small country to apprentice themselves to you. This didn't seem to bother Joshua, who we can be sure had ambitions of his own. Moses called him a servant for good reason (Josh. 1:16). No wonder he saw something in this guy!

Joshua was put in charge of the tabernacle, assisting Moses in the daily organizing and administering of the spiritual life of the budding nation (Exod. 33:11). He also became the commanding general of the tribal armies. Moses spent a great deal of time with Joshua, often reciting their history to him and the lessons they had learned (Exod. 17:14). Joshua was one of twelve spies chosen to reconnoiter the promised land and only one of two that brought back a good report—something that did not set well with his contemporaries (Num. 14:6–9). What a training program! Eventually Joshua took over and led the invasion of the promised land after Moses had passed away (Deut. 31:14, 23).

Joshua's passion was for the things of God—the things the friend of God, Moses, had invested in him—and for the people who hungered for a home for forty years wandering in the wilderness. He did not seek his own, and his ambition was always for others.

The right kind of ambition is both moral and spiritual. Morality by nature is speculative, meaning that there are no universally accepted standards, no laboratory observations that will brand your morality as correct. It is not a matter of science. Standards of conduct, for example, become relative to the society producing them. To be effective, a person's morality must be a reflection of his or her values, and these values must incorporate more than the societal norms producing them. They must also include a desire to improve one's self in a manner that contributes to the betterment of the whole.

For a believer, morality is based in an absolute standard; and though society does influence our standards of conduct they ultimately are rooted in Scripture. "This Book of the Law shall not depart from your mouth, but you shall meditate in it day and night, that you may observe to do according to all that is written in it. For then you will make your way prosperous, and then you will have good success" (Josh. 1:8). If my morality reflects my values, and these values are rooted in Scripture, then I will naturally put the interests of others before my own.

Personal ambition that is a demonstration of love is more than simply believing in axioms like "do not kill," "do not commit adultery," or just keeping the rest of the Ten Commandments. In the organizational story in the preceding chapter, who acted in a morally appropriate manner? Was it top management facing change or middle management insisting on change?

Playing the "ambition card" was not a good moral decision. It protected and advanced the position of a few at the expense of the group and to the detriment of the organization. Was it a decision within the authority of those who made it? Certainly. Was it a decision that was wrong to make? Who is to say? Was it a decision consistent with the culture and a societal norm within that culture? Yes, it was. But it still was morally wrong. It violates kingdom values rooted in biblical principle (e.g., Phil. 2:3–7).

The decisions I regret most in life, both professionally and personally, were ones made in vested self-interest. Inevitably they have wounded my career and left alienation in their wake. The one thing they all have in common is a moral element. I chose *me* instead of *us*. This is true for all of us, a part of our humanity.

I am more concerned with the tenor of my life. What is the pattern? Am I more often consistently choosing the better path to take, or is my ambition more consistently focused on me? Authenticity demands that I strive for an ambition for things that are bigger than myself and reconciliation for those exceptions where it is not bigger.

Gary and I were part of the same work group. We tended to confide in one another somewhat more freely than the rest of the team since we were both struggling in our roles, not quite sure if the new boss was going to keep us on or let us go. A number of our former teammates had already left or been asked to leave. You can understand our insecurity and strong desire to do well.

Gary confided some information in me and asked that I keep it confidential. The very next day I failed him! In a conversation at the lunch table, I let slip pass my lips a key piece of information. I didn't spill all the beans, but I did violate his confidentiality. It was not a loving thing to do to a teammate, and when he heard about it, he turned up in my office first thing the following morning really ticked. My ambition got away from me. I wanted to be the big man with the big news, and I let Gary down.

Immediately recognizing my folly, I asked Gary's forgiveness, which he was gracious enough to give. I then went back to everyone at the table, told them the story—much to my embarrassment, and asked for their forgiveness. Since this was a secular workplace, some acted with surprise, some understood, and all forgave me. I completed my act of reconciliation by circling back with Gary and letting him know what I had done. Without that closure I am sure Gary would not be as willing to trust me again in the future. In this case we continued to be good friends supporting each other in the workplace.

It is the little things like a broken confidence that trip us up, often revealing where our ambitions truly lie. Frankly, I struggled with the idea of going back to those at the table. It was easy to think everything was all right simply because I had made it right with Gary. But that would not have been love the way Paul described it in terms of not seeking your own.

Love does not seek its own. It is OK to be ambitious, guys. In fact, we need ambition to make something of ourselves, achieve something worthwhile. Ambition is not a sin. Paul used a reflexive pronoun here, pointing back at us. When we seek to accomplish something just for ourselves in the context of our relationship with others, we become manipulators; and people around us feel used. This is love directed inwardly and not exclusive love—love that excludes "me" from the equation.

Jesus was ambitious. He set out to redeem all creation. He did it! But it took everything he had to love us that way.

Philippians 2:5–7 (NASB) says he "emptied Himself" on our behalf. So ask yourself: are you ambitious for that next promotion because it means living up to your God-designed potential, expanding your opportunities to contribute, increasing your capacity to serve, enabling you to be a better steward of your family, and freeing up time and resources to invest in the kingdom? Or do you just like the title and the money that goes with it? It is a challenging question that we may not answer the same way every day.

Wally faced the same challenge every day and came out on top because he chose more often than not to be selfless in his ambition. Married more than sixty-four years to the same woman, Wally and Betty have raised a wonderful family of highly successful children. I know—I married their daughter.

We spend most Sundays together going to church, eating lunch out, and playing cards. Retired now, they have their small-group Bible study, neighborhood friends, and family for company and encouragement. At eighty-three, Wally is still the encourager.

Hanging around them you would never know Wally was a decorated WWII pilot shot down over Germany, captured by the Russians, and smuggled back to do it all over again. He almost beat the letter home that told Mom he was a POW. In later years he worked his way through school and became a successful businessman. In time he owned his own company, a foundry, and well into his seventies was still climbing down mine shafts and up inside blast furnaces. His ambition for his family produced fame and fortune for himself in his own generation, but those things were not his goal.

His ambition was to be a good husband and father. Those other things were spin-offs, just tertiary results that never were his focus. I am grateful to be a beneficiary of the world he changed with his love.

What is it that moves us to have a passion for others? King David had a passion for others that sometimes got the best of him. He lamented these failings in Psalm 51 as he expressed his remorse and longing to be restored to a right relationship with God and with others. His innermost thoughts in this passage provide a checklist for us.

1. When someone has wronged you, do you respond in mercy, or do you demand justice? (For David's perspective, see Ps. 51:1–4.)

2. When you have wronged someone, do you seek to make it right on the outside, or do you go further to genuinely seek to be different on the inside? (David sought change from the inside out, see Ps. 51:5–9.)

3. When your character is in question, do you persist in seeking the truth about yourself, or do you want to move on quickly, putting the problem behind you? (David sought to learn from his mistakes, not run from them, see Ps. 51:10–13.)

4. When no one but you knows you have blown it, are you broken in spirit, or do you persist in maintaining the perception that you are right? (David was broken in spirit, see Ps. 51:14–17.)

5. How long are you willing to live looking good on the outside without true inward renewal? (David pleased God because of true inward renewal, see Ps. 51:18–19.)

Genuine renewal is tough work. It requires the ultimate in not seeking your own. It requires an end to self-protective behavior. Boy, do I hate that! For a man, exposure is the kiss of death! I would rather you just not like me than get to see my bad stuff (because then you would really not like me). It is easier for guys to move on and leave a damaged relationship in their wake than it is to go back to the lunch table.

I recently had a conversation with a well-known Christian leader who, like King David, committed adultery some years ago. The consequences of his act cost him his ministry; many friends abandoned the relationship they had shared for many years. He was pilloried in the press. Some in his faith community preferred to shoot the wounded rather than help with the healing, and whatever family life he had went up in smoke.

Now the family is back together, and he is once again engaged in meaningful ministry. Nothing like it was in the old days, but certainly a credit to success on the road to recovery.

What struck me as I listened was the enormous pain that the process of recovering from selfish ambition and seeking your own had created in this person's life. Laid open to his very soul for all to see, this committed Christian was still working through issues with a level of transparency most are not capable of mustering up. His courage in learning to love the way God designed us to love, and leaving behind what the world tells us about love, now inspires men across the nation to fight the good fight even when every instinct we have tells us to shut up!

Love that does not seek its own will push us on to new understandings of the role of appropriate vulnerability and transparency in our lives as men and require us to come to grips with humility. There was a lot that happened to this person that made him think about giving up, bailing out on the recovery process of restoration and reconciliation. Being treated like a loser, damaged goods, is enough to provoke anyone. However, love is not provoked; and because he chose not to seek his own and not to be provoked, his world and—praise God—the world of his restored family is forever different.

Chapter Eight

———◆———

Key 6: Is Not Provoked, Part I

H ere are three stories that have something in common.

Homer, the Greek poet, is said to have committed suicide for a singular and strange reason in one version of his life's story. As the legend goes, he met some boys coming home from a fishing trip. When he inquired as to their luck, they responded with a riddle. What we caught we threw away and what we didn't catch we have. Homer's inability to understand they were referring to fleas so provoked him that he killed himself.

Rudolph Kreutzer was a famous composer and acquaintance of Beethoven. It is this same Kreutzer that Beethoven's famous sonata for violin and piano, Opus 47, is named for, the "Kreutzer Sonata." Kreutzer's good fortune in being memorialized this way came about quite by happenstance. Beethoven never intended to name the sonata after him but after another young colleague named Bridgetower. However, before the sonata was published, Beethoven and Bridgetower quarreled over a young lady. Their friendship ended, and Bridgetower's name was removed from the title page.

Abraham Lincoln met Edwin Stanton when they were both practicing law. Stanton had no patience for Lincoln. In their first case facing each other in court, he derided Lincoln's appearance, demanded he be removed from the courtroom, and otherwise ignored him. Lincoln's client lost the case, and Stanton won for his client. Years later when Lincoln was president of the United States, he chose Stanton, who was still an outspoken critic, to be his secretary of war because he had a brilliant mind.

During the Civil War, as one general after another was replaced, Stanton came to Lincoln in an explosion about one particular general who wasn't cutting it. He angrily stated he was going to write the general and share with him all he had just unloaded on the president. Lincoln encouraged him to do so. In two days Stanton brought the letter back and read it to Lincoln, who thanked Stanton and told him to throw the letter away. Its purpose had been served. It took two days to write, and Stanton had cooled off by then.

What these stories have in common, beyond the fact that they are stories about men with name recognition, is that they describe being provoked to angry action in the sense Paul talked about in the phrase "is not provoked." In one case that provocation comes from within as an expression of frustration. In another case the provocation comes from circumstances— the guy doesn't get the girl. In the third instance the provocation comes from trying to change the unchangeable. We will often encounter those situations that provoke us whether it is a result of an internal struggle, the circumstances we face, or things we are powerless to change. Sooner or later we will explode in angry words or deeds as well.

There are some situations I cannot handle as well as others. When I find myself in these circumstances, I really want to explode, get in someone's face, and just let him have it! These may not be the same triggers that set you off, but here are a few that really get my goat:

Someone makes up his or her mind about me or about something I have done without getting the whole story. He or she seems ready just to write me off. "He who answers a matter before he hears it, it is folly and shame to him" (Prov. 18:13). The idea here is to get the whole story before you start running your mouth.

Speaking of running your mouth, here is another big bugaboo. People who blab bad news to the world-at-large, regardless of its veracity. "A prudent man conceals knowledge, But the heart of fools proclaims foolishness" (Prov. 12:23). It is better to conceal dishonor, real or imagined, from the world-at-large than it is to spread it about. This Scripture and other passages addressing the same idea are not asking us to sweep sin under the rug. The admonition is to keep your mouth shut if you are not actively involved as part of the solution to the problem.

Then there are the "gotchas"! These people lie in wait, looking for that one piece of information that is going to make you smaller and them bigger; and when it comes along—gotcha! Christians are really good at this when legalism becomes a substitute for spiritual maturity.

Now here is my problem. When the conversation turns to these kinds of unloving, self-righteous personalities—consuming bad news like it was manna from heaven to be shared with others—I must also realize that the conversation is about me. I am sometimes unloving in these ways also. I have stepped over the pharisaical line and spoken of things inappropriately out of self-interest as well. For guys, this can be a subtle trap. We like to measure ourselves against others; and no matter how short we may be in our own eyes, if someone is less in stature, then we are OK.

The other problem here is the temper. Why does it fry my socks more than at other times when these things happen to me? Anger as a choice and not just a feeling erupts from subliminal places deep in our longings. It can signal a blocked goal, disappointed expectation, or frustrated desire. What are my goals when these explosions occur? Frankly, to be seen as competent and adequate, to be liked and admired. These are not wrong desires, guys. God made us to be heroes. It is just that sin gets in the way; and when I look bad (especially when it is not deserved), I can get really angry.

This is what Paul was talking about when he said love is not provoked. In fact, it is the same root word as *anger*. If we are going to love exclusively, we have to give up being irritable; and even though anger may emerge from time to time, make sure it is not an unrighteous anger and never boils over. Making this a reality is tough, tough, tough—especially when the real problem may be simply that my pride has been pricked. The antidote for that is a lasting dose of humility.

Like ambition, this is another misunderstood and mis-used term in Christian circles. However, men need both ambition and humility in large quantities; and we will spend, therefore, a little extra time elevating the value of humility as a wonderful male steroid, potentially even more powerful than testosterone. So we don't take this too personally, men, let's start with a feminine illustration.

Janet is my friend. She is, or at least was, a certified spin-ster. Now most women would object to that label. However, Janet tells her own story with great humor as a part of the train-ing she provides for presidents, CEOs, board chairs, and other corporate luminaries who come to her for advice. Let me tell you about Janet before I tell you her story.

Janet worked hard her entire life to get ahead. She is focused, hardworking, and successful. She got her master's degree and her doctorate on her own later in life. That means she also had to work to support herself. When I met Janet, she was the dean of education for a local college. Smart, energetic, fun, and savvy, she cut a wide swath among her peers and was no one's pushover.

The day eventually came when Janet got married. She was, well, getting hitched a little later in life than the statistical norm, let's say. Janet and her fiancé were sailing around the Caribbean and had planned their wedding on one of the islands. When they appeared at the minister of justice's offices, Janet learned she would need a wedding license. When she appeared at the Wedding License Bureau down the street, she discovered on the application a category called "condition" that she was required to fill out.

There were only three "conditions" to choose from: widow, divorced, or spinster. Janet was neither widowed nor divorced and was not about to choose spinster! Of course, an argument with the official ensued with Janet finally shouting at the official, "I am a doctor and a dean, and you cannot make me say I am a spinster!" To her soon-to-be (maybe) husband on his knees weeping with laughter, she said, "I love you dearly; but if I have to say I am a spinster, you are going to stay single!" Sometime later the problem was resolved. Janet believed no one would ever see the marriage license and her "condition," so she swallowed her pride and filled out the form. Too bad her assumption was wrong.

When they returned to the United States and Janet returned to work, she went to personnel administration at the college to add her new husband to her health benefits plan. Guess what they wanted to see? You got it—a copy of her marriage license. Guess how long it took for her "condition" to be leaked all over the school? (About as long it takes light to reach the earth from the sun.) Now everyone knew she was a legally certified spinster with a document to prove it! Janet was still a doctor and a dean, but now a little less full of herself and a little more in touch with reality.

Janet tells this story in her leadership seminars to help the participants leave their titles and their attitudes at the door. She is interested in building perspective into the lives of these leaders and not promoting their personalities. Having worked with Janet for some time now, I can safely say she has the right perspective on humility. Many people fear this quality because they believe it will lead to being humiliated, being treated like a doormat, and ultimately kept in the background—in other words, keep them from getting ahead. Just the opposite is true. True humility builds the respect and admiration of others.

The opposite of humility is self-conceit. It is not conceit to take pride in ourselves, our family, our work, our country, and all that is worthy of our best. Humility is attained by aiming at the highest we know with the utmost we have while knowing we all come short of the mark. This is part of what makes true humility attractive to others. The single guy who comes across to the opposite sex as spiritually mature and healthy in his ambition and humility isn't going to need cologne to turn heads.

Humility is a commitment to seek the interests of others, sometimes over your own, and is not acquired pragmatically. It is not something you do. It is something you are. Humility requires a certain perspective, mind-set, and maturity and is an element of our character. That is why insincere apologies, disingenuous acceptance of responsibility, and withholding forgiveness are never sensed by others as humility on your part. That is why it takes more than an apology to restore a relationship—and guys like to think if they have gone through the act of apologizing it ought to be accepted, and they wonder why in the world everything just can't go back to normal!

Humility enables you to listen without constructing your own argument at the same time. Humility enables you to validate someone else's feelings without agreeing. Humility enables you to accept responsibility without shifting blame to others. Humility enables you to have a long fuse that never quite gets to the explosion.

Some personalities are like sandpaper and a match. Without humility the best you can hope for is managing the relationship so the two never rub together. Choosing to exercise character—humility—opens the door for change. Pride, on the other hand, makes us easily bruised. So we become self-protective and expect others to adjust to us.

We label the word *humility* as weakness to excuse our lack of choice when, indeed, it is the greatest position of strength we can take. Why? Because it takes strength to let others be human, strength to adjust to their needs, and strength not to insist on what you may view as your rights. Humility does not make assumptions about others—their motives, feelings, and thoughts—and then marginalize them. Humility treats others with respect regardless of their state. Humility is always about who you are, not who the other person is or is not.

According to Albert Einstein, "No amount of experimentation can ever prove me right; a single experiment can prove me wrong." Helen Keller believed her chief duty was to accomplish humble tasks as if they were great and noble. Mahatma

Gandhi knew it was healthy to be reminded that the strongest might weaken and the wisest might err, and so it is unwise to be too sure of one's own wisdom. What these three great people have in common in these perspectives is an understanding of the personal impacts of humility. A lack of humility can keep great things from happening in our world.

Don't be quick-tempered, easily provoked (Eccl. 7:8–9). Instead, focus on God's perspective, "If My people who are called by My name will humble themselves, and pray and seek My face, and turn from their wicked ways, then I will hear from heaven, and will forgive their sin and heal their land" (2 Chron. 7:14).

I got to know Staff Sergeant Wilson at my last duty station just before I left active duty. He taught basic refrigeration mechanics to young marines just out of boot camp and infantry training. They would be reassigned to the fleet as heating, ventilation, and air-conditioning specialists once their course of instruction was completed. Sergeant Wilson was a career marine and had just finished an overseas tour. He was looking forward to a few years stateside with his wife and two children in a comfortable teaching assignment.

That morning he and his wife shared some strong words over breakfast. Sergeant Wilson got worked up, jumped up, and stormed out the door. Since they lived on base, it was only a few minutes before he was at work. Running a little late because the conversation had taken a little longer, he arrived to find the young marines already seated in the classroom comprised of a large open bay with a half dozen rows of workbenches at one end and a small set of bleachers in front of the central open area at the other end. (For some reason marines love bleachers.)

Sergeant Wilson strode purposefully in, "GOOD MORNING, CLASS!"

They snapped to attention and shouted back, "GOOD MORNING, STAFF SERGEANT!"

"At ease, men," Sergeant Wilson commanded. When they were seated, he went on, "Today we are going to learn how to charge a system with refrigerant." With that he moved a few paces into the cleared area where a compressor and all the equipment needed to charge the system with refrigerant had been set up, and then turned on the compressor.

As he stood there beginning the lecture, the compressor exploded and took off the top half of his head. It seems in his distracted hurry, none of the safety devices had been turned on. That's when they called me.

Less than an hour after he had left his wife at the breakfast table, I was knocking on their door with the chaplain and our commanding officer. Love is not provoked; and when it is, the consequences may be everlasting. Fortunately, that is not always the case. There are several lessons in this dramatic story.

1. Anger and humility are seldom partners.
2. When you are provoked to anger, others certainly may be hurt but not nearly as much as you may hurt yourself.
3. Sometimes the consequences of our angry actions are not reversible.

Grandchildren are such great lesson makers. We have the treat of spending time with our grandchildren on a regular basis. Sometimes they come to stay with us. During those extended visits we get to see their development in action. At three, they are inquisitive about everything, have more undirected energy than probably at any other time in life, and are exploring their world. That's a really nice grandparent way of saying they are pushing the envelope, trying our patience, and generally out of control.

Reining them in constructively is an exercise in patience and self-control. We have come to realize we are better at it now than we were the first time around. I think I am far less easily provoked now than I was when their parents were their age. (Of course, we only had cloth diapers then, and that is enough to drive any man over the edge!) The point is, the things my kids used to do that would wear me down and produce an angry outburst don't do that anymore. Perhaps I am more self-aware. Hopefully, I have matured and learned a few things about not being provoked. I know I sure do love my grandchildren.

Chapter Nine

Key 6: Is Not Provoked, Part II

Part of the reason we can be easily provoked is simply a lack of self-awareness. I really don't know when I am acting like a spoiled brat most of the time, and my generous opinion of myself can be unsupported by the facts. In reality, most of us do not perceive ourselves at the extremes of behavior but rather more pleasantly in between.

Self-awareness is difficult, and being objective about what we see even tougher. Here is a little test to illustrate the point. Think of people you know at work or in your neighborhood or even in your family. How do you experience them? What is the message they send regarding humility? Each of the following descriptive statements captures a characteristic attitude or behavior associated with humility. When I took this assessment, I had someone specific in mind when I read each of the statements. You can see that I marked each statement on a scale from one (least) to five (most) as to whether this description was more or less representative of this person. You can find the score at the bottom of the table.

Quality	Score				
	Least Like		Most Like		
	1	2	3	4	5
This individual enjoys a great deal of self-respect.			X		
This individual demonstrates an appreciation for the contribution of others.		X			
This individual rarely displays an arrogant attitude.			X		
This individual is able to laugh at himself.				X	
This individual is a good listener and rarely interrupts.	X				
This individual is not a micromanager but believes in enabling the success of others.	X				
This individual has an open mind.		X			
This individual solicits feedback and accepts criticism well.	X				
This individual does not "toot his own horn" very much.				X	
This individual relates to others with an appropriate transparency and vulnerability.				X	
Sub Totals	3	4	6	12	0
Grand Total					25

In the previous scenario, I scored the person observed a twenty-five out of a possible fifty. Being perceived as having an average amount of humility would seem to be a good thing. However, the higher the score, the better the odds are you will be less easily provoked in your relationships with others. Notice that one of the factors helping this "average" person is that he doesn't toot his own horn much. At the same time this person scores low on being open to criticism, believing in others, and being a good listener. So being average isn't necessarily a good thing!

How would you feel if you were this person and I came to you with this feedback? "You know, Wayne, I really appreciate the fact that you don't take yourself too seriously and can laugh at yourself. I respect you for not acting arrogantly and not always trying to one-up others with your accomplishments. But I have to say that you really are not a good listener, you are always running over people in conversation, and you don't have a real open attitude about criticism. In fact, you make it clear 'that dog doesn't hunt.'"

Which of these two sets of comments are you most likely to receive? Which are you more willing to accept as accurate descriptions of your behavior or attitudes? See what I mean? It's tough to have an accurate self-appraisal when it comes to our hot buttons and what provokes us easily.

When I sat down with Wayne (not his real name) and provided this feedback, I got instant agreement on the positive and nothing but arguments designed to minimize on the negative. Wayne really believed he was more open than I perceived him to be. The problem was that Wayne's world was full of people who saw him just the way I did and qualified their relationship with him accordingly. What keeps Wayne from sufficient humility to embrace reality?

On the face of it, people lacking in humility cannot afford to let others take risks that may reflect upon them negatively even if they themselves are risk takers. If, as a person, you tend to be like Wayne and don't regularly solicit and respond to feedback, you have another reason for not letting others take risks: it puts outcomes out of your control. Out of control, looking bad—two things we hate as men. The larger problem is not just what this does to our capacity to love but the impact on our families, our neighborhoods, and our careers. The problem is compounded because without risk taking there is no creativity.

People like Wayne may have no problem with their own creativity but may have big problems with other creative people who make them look bad or cannot be controlled. Where there is little creativity and no real consensus, there is also little cooperation. Frustration, anger, irritation, and dissatisfaction will periodically characterize relationships either because they have been provoked or they have provoked others.

Wayne's career prospects are limited. He has irritated enough people in the right places that he is nonpromotable. Now he is trapped between little chance for career advancement and insufficient reason to be terminated. Easily provoked and lacking humility—not a nice world.

At this point my heart is agreeing, and my mind is rebelling. Everything I understand about humility and its relationship to being easily provoked up to this point rings true. Knowing that I cannot keep all of this information in a state of readiness to use when I am tempted to be less than humble and slow to anger frustrates me! How do I make the Scriptures work for me on this issue? How do I remember to be humble?

We need to step back and get a larger perspective.

"I will instruct you and teach you in the way you should go; I will guide you with My eye" (Ps. 32:8). "The way you should go" refers to the best pathway for your life. The more I listen to God, the more effective I will be in everything, including cultivating a humble spirit. God wants to guide me. I just have to give him the opportunity. For me this means two simple things: asking for a chance to choose my pathway and giving myself reminders that keep things in perspective. Here's what I mean.

I ask the Lord to use the Holy Spirit to put a hitch in my giddy-up when I am about to think or do the wrong thing—just a simple attention-getting pause that will give me a chance to choose to change my thinking or do something differently than I was planning to do. You know it works! Just that simple hiccup in time that the Holy Spirit brings is enough to reconsider where I am going and choose a different pathway, God's pathway. It has made an enormous difference in my world.

It has meant holding my tongue when teasing was about to go too far, not lashing out when a stinging comment cut too close to the bone, or not looking a second time when an underdressed overexposed young lady passed by. It has meant listening a little longer when I have been tempted to jump in, considering what may be best for the other person rather than what I want, or waiting for another to praise me rather than be heard praising myself. Above all, it has given me a longer fuse and helped remove angry explosions from my life. Do I ever get it wrong? You bet, all the time, but living otherwise has become so enjoyable it is easy to get back on the right pathway.

Reminders were the second "simple thing" mentioned that help me keep things in perspective. We all need reminders now and then that keep our sense of self-importance in balance.

I have a picture stored away that I come across from time to time. Thirteen young men, many barely out of their teens, looking full of themselves in their military uniforms headed for Vietnam. Not too many months after that graduation picture was taken, some of them were dead.

My father, his body weakened by alcoholism, died of pneumonia in midlife. My mother passed prematurely due to cancer. One of my best friends, after a twenty-year career in the Air Force, augered into the ground in a rare commercial airline accident, the cause of which is still not positively known today.

I am reminded that there is no escape from ultimate circumstances, whether they come into our lives as a result of war, disease, illness, accident, or just poor choices. It is humbling to know that it could have been me, and still might be, in those scenarios and that no amount of talent, skill, education, or achievement will in the end deliver me from death. The reality that, in some sense, I am subject to the circumstances of life just like anyone else helps me keep in perspective my smallness.

That can be pretty depressing if that is all there is to life. You are born. Stuff happens. You die. You may be able to improve the quality of the journey from the cradle to the grave with careful planning, diligent effort, and a little luck; but the outcome remains the same. As a man, when I am reminded of my smallness, I resent it until I am reminded as well of God's greatness and his promise to me.

"And we know that all things work together for good to those who love God, to those who are the called according to His purpose" (Rom. 8:28). When I am seeking his pathways, God promises to make sure the outcome of circumstances in my life is good no matter how bad they may be otherwise.

Wow! When the Holy Spirit gives me an opportunity to love exclusively and I choose this pathway, even in the smallest thought or action, God is going to take charge of the outcome. Wow! Though my smallness in the grand scheme of things may keep me humble, God thinks I am important enough to keep an eye on me, guide me, and change the world through me.

Smallness is truly greatness. We just don't recognize it at times. Telemachus was a fifth-century monk who lived in a monastery in what is now Turkey. At one point in his life he decided to go to Rome. When he got to Rome, he ran into crowds on their way to the Coliseum and followed them in. Thousands upon thousands of people had gathered for the gladiator games. These men would fight each other and animals to death in the amphitheater for the pleasure of the crowd.

Telemachus left his seat and climbed into the ring and stood between two gladiators shouting, "In the name of Christ, stop!" This went on until, the crowd jeering, one of the gladiators knocked him to the ground.

Telemachus got up and continued his interference, all the while shouting, "In the name of Christ, stop!"

The crowd began to demand his death. One of the gladiators obliged them, running Telemachus through with his sword.

Telemachus fell to the ground and bled to death with the cry still on his lips, "In the name of Christ, stop!"

The crowd was silenced. One by one, and then in groups, everyone left the Coliseum. Three days later the emperor ended the games by decree. This was the last gladiatorial contest in history. Telemachus was provoked but not to anger. His act of humility changed his world forever and changed history.

Our acts of humility will seldom be as dramatic, but they can be just as far-reaching. When we let go of the need to be right in an argument, when we take the initiative to apologize, when we choose not to criticize but encourage instead, these have far-reaching consequences in the lives of those we love. When we choose not to shout, when we choose to let the other go first, when we choose not to insist on doing things our way, others find new freedom to excel that we would otherwise take away from them. When we choose to serve rather than be served, when we choose to expose ourselves to criticism and ridicule because we are doing the right thing, when we choose not to retaliate, we set a profound example for those we serve.

When lived consistently, all of these choices have a lasting impact on those around us that we may never see or measure—but it is there nonetheless. Children are wonderful examples of how much power we have to mark someone else for life without ever knowing it. What a blessing indeed it is to be marked by someone's humility rather than scarred by someone's anger.

Douglas has few childhood memories earlier than eight or nine years of age. Now at age thirty-seven, he has trouble controlling his emotions. Douglas is way too easily provoked and originally was referred for anger management training by his employer. In addition, Douglas can be moody, given to the blues, has difficulty concentrating or remembering things, and has a low startle threshold. When it was noticed that most of his outbursts at work were brought on by the stress of deadlines and not interactions with other employees, the counselor began to suspect more than just trouble managing anger.

During the first two years of life, our brains are developing more rapidly than at other times. This is particularly true of the areas of the brain involved in emotional development, the hippocampus and prefrontal cortex. By the time a child is seven or eight, the frontal lobes are developing rapidly. This is where conceptualizing takes place so that by the time a child is twelve or fifteen, he can separate himself from his world enough so that everything that goes on around him isn't subliminally understood by him to be his fault.

During these years there are sensitive windows of development where the lack of stimulation or the wrong kind of stimulation in the child's environment can affect neurological development. The right kind of experience, for example, would include the nurturing touch of a loving parent. The wrong kind of experience, for example, would include parents constantly shouting at each other, a mom constantly criticizing her son for being a crybaby, or a dad who verbally or physically abuses mom in front of the child.

Douglas had far too much of this kind of exposure in his formative years. Now, as an adult, he was acting like a victim of posttraumatic stress disorder. The manner in which he processes stimuli in the workplace related to pressing deadlines causes a predictable emotional response reflecting patterns laid down long ago during his neurological development. Instead of twelve weeks of brief therapy, Douglas is looking at five to eight years of physiological and psychological change on the road back to healthy responses to life's tougher circumstances.

Mom and dad came from a generation where they "let it all hang out." When they were provoked, they went right to nuclear warfare. Unfortunately, the abuse and neglect scarred Douglas for life. Better our children are marked by our humility than our anger. Love is not provoked.

My earliest childhood memories go back to about nine months of age. That does not mean I am any healthier than Douglas is. I do remember a loving and nurturing setting in the early years that was very quiet (except for my older brother and me crashing around the house). I tend not to be provoked easily and credit that to patterns established in those early years and not to some maturity on my part. My dysfunctional responses tend to be passive-aggressive, more consistent with being the second son in birth order.

Though it is clear our formative years have a great deal to do with our ability to be humble when it comes to provocation, to loving others, those experiences do not excuse bad behavior or guarantee good behavior. Adam and Eve had the perfect parent and still made bad choices with inevitable and inescapable consequences. Men, it is all about choice when it comes to loving others the way God designed us best to love. Our histories can inform us about the obstacles we may need to work on, but they are not deterministic. We can choose not to be provoked, and because of that choice, the world we share with those we love can be a better place.

Chapter Ten

Key 7: Thinks No Evil

Thinks no evil. This simple phrase is loaded with content. Other versions of the Bible translate this phrase in 1 Corinthians 13:5 as "keeps no record of wrongs" (NIV), "does not take into account a wrong suffered" (NASB), or "doesn't keep score of the sins of others" (*The Message*). It seems a bit confusing. For example, how do they get the idea of counting out of the word "thinks"?

Imagine yourself in the grocery store. It's Friday and you have stopped on your way home from work to pick up some things for a barbecue. There are guests coming so you have a special menu in mind but a limited budget. So, as you walk the aisles, you are planning alternatives to the menu as various options on the shelves trigger your thinking. You mentally keep tabs on the price of each item, discarding the more expensive ones as you go. Within twenty minutes you are at the cash register with a menu slightly different from the one you had in mind when you walked in but well within your budget for the event. Sure enough, the cash register total confirms that your running tally was right on target.

This is the concept that connects the word *think* with the word *account* or *record*. It originally was a term of commercial use describing the act or thought of giving value or assigning worth to something as a part of planning. Paul used the same word in other places to describe people who judge others unfairly, draw conclusions based on assumptions, or dismiss others out of hand as having no value. The point here is that we should not allow ourselves to think that way.

Paul went to some lengths to load up this phrase to impress upon us the importance of not harboring bad thoughts about other people. The specific evil he had in mind is the way in which we can label others as bad people in our minds and keep a mental list of their offenses handy. Paul used this same word for evil in other places talking about slanderers, liars, and arrogant people that keep track of wrongs in order to tear people down.

If we understand the comparison correctly, what Paul was saying is that "thinks no evil" means we do not practice tearing others down when we should be giving them the benefit of the doubt and building them up. This is easier to say than to do. Rusty is a case in point.

Rusty is one of those career-climbing blowhards everyone loves to hate. Prideful, selfish, I found him to be especially irritating when he orchestrates his own public recognition for accomplishments that should be attributed to others. When he steals my thunder, it is especially galling, and I find myself holding a grudge and keeping track of all of his other failings as well.

Once when I was bad-mouthing Rusty to a friend (OK, so I've already made two mistakes—keeping track of perceived wrongs and talking behind his back), I got some advice I am forever grateful for. What may or may not happen to Rusty is of no consequence to me. God is in charge of how I get ahead. "Do not lift up your horn on high; Do not speak with a stiff neck. For exaltation comes neither from the east nor from the west nor from the south. But God is the Judge: He puts down one, and exalts another" (Ps. 75:5–7).

My problem was that I was too impatient, too intolerant, and too jealous of good things that happened to other people. There are only so many promotions to go around, only so many awards to win, and only so much recognition to be had. Every time someone else gets these things, it means less opportunity for me to get noticed and get ahead. This does seem immature, doesn't it? But men, we can all be like this. It is our instinct to compete either passively or actively. For too many of us, this means climbing over the backs of others to get ahead.

God does not want us to live this way. Promotion does not come inevitably from our employer. Recognition does not ultimately come from our peers or professional societies. It all ultimately comes from the Lord. Until I learn this truth, I am helpless to love others I perceive as getting in my way. However, understanding does not become conviction until it is successfully tested in the crucible of daily living.

So, even to this day, when I am offended by someone else's egocentric conduct I remind myself that God is in control and releasing the fear that he is not, find myself with a new capacity to be gracious and kind. His faithfulness demonstrated time and again only strengthens my commitment not to be the kind of person who is willing to believe the worst about people and keep a record of their wrongs.

Why is it that we are the way we are? Why do the Rustys of the world get my goat? What is it about our instinct to compete that sends our thinking first to the dark side so much of the time? Well, it is in our nature. Jeremiah captured this tension between good and evil in us so poetically in Jeremiah 17:5–10.

Thus says the LORD:
"Cursed is the man who trusts in man
And makes flesh his strength,
Whose heart departs from the LORD.
For he shall be like a shrub in the desert,
And shall not see when good comes,
But shall inhabit the parched places in the wilderness,
In a salt land which is not inhabited.
Blessed is the man who trusts in the LORD,
And whose hope is the LORD.
For he shall be like a tree planted by the waters,
Which spreads out its roots by the river,
And will not fear when heat comes;
But its leaf will be green,
And will not be anxious in the year of drought,
Nor will cease from yielding fruit.
The heart is deceitful above all things,
And desperately wicked;
Who can know it?
I, the LORD, search the heart,
I test the mind,
Even to give every man according to his ways,
According to the fruit of his doings."

The person who trusts in his own wisdom and strength to get ahead is contrasted with the person who has placed his hope and trust in God. Then they are compared in the same way—both types of people can be tricked by their own hearts into thinking and behaving poorly. It is only the Lord who can truly see into the depths of our motivations. Loving others is not automatic. It is a choice every single day.

Paul talked about this kind of choice in Galatians 6:10: "Therefore, as we have opportunity, let us do good to all." Rusty made this choice, much to everyone's surprise.

Every year where Rusty and I worked, customer service awards were given. It was a big deal, celebrated with an awards dinner, plaques, speeches, pictures with the CEO, the whole nine yards. Every year Rusty had himself nominated by someone whom he nominated in turn. Some of us suspected he went after multiple nominations. Then he schmoozed the judges. Most years it worked.

When the leadership team met that year to validate the judges' final picks, Rusty interrupted the discussion and asked that his name be taken off the list. He had come to the conclusion that this was an employee award and managers should not even be considered. Well, I had to reframe my thinking about Rusty, especially since his behavior after that reflected the same consistent change in attitude. When I asked him about the change, here is what I heard:

> I found out the hard way that when I take credit for things other people have done there comes a time when people expect me actually to be able to accomplish what I took credit for! Those times when my word was found lacking left me feeling empty. My wife pointed out to me during a bout of flagrant self-promotion that I was a real pain in the buttocks to live with, and she was actively considering moving out. That got my attention.

> When I started letting go, I realized that my attention-getting behavior really didn't help. It actually

hurt my relationships with others and didn't get me ahead like I thought it would. When I kept my mouth shut, I discovered things went much better; and when I actually praised others, I ended up with the recognition I was trying to force. My world is filled with a whole lot less anxiety as a result.

Well, as I said, I had to reframe my thinking about Rusty as well—and not just Rusty but anyone I was tempted to think poorly of—because, in the long run, it made me feel better about myself. These kinds of personal failures all have a weight to them. When added up, they become a heavy burden. Rusty obviously experienced a new freedom when he chose to accept responsibility, admit his failure, and press on again with a new attitude.

One of the lessons I learned early in my career was that you often are remembered best for your last biggest mistake. Coupled with an instinct to compete, this meant for me failure was something to be avoided, if not in actuality then at least in appearance. Yet failure is life's greatest university. In the last half of Proverbs 1, Solomon described how wisdom shouts in the streets, the marketplace, the home—all places where life's ups and downs take place. Failure from this perspective is an inescapable ingredient of daily living.

If I am to refuse to think evil of others, I must also choose to embrace the inevitability of failing in this effort. So how does one cope with failure? First, I have to ignore my instinct to hide. Next I have to choose to deny my competitive nature and the temptation to look good at the expense of others. Then I need to accept responsibility for my thoughts and actions; and finally I must choose to move forward, by the grace of God, with a different attitude.

Accepting responsibility is difficult at times because it is so easy to shift responsibility elsewhere. My parents were successful professionals. They were very loving, but in their later years they also yelled a lot. Failure to live up to their expectations sometimes produced yelling; yelling produced fear; fear produced anger; and anger produced inappropriate behavior on my part. A part of me wants to say my bad behavior was their fault and that I was just responding in the way they set me up to respond.

As a teenager I had no understanding of how appropriately to deal with the fear and frustration I was feeling, so I was just acting out. Sounds reasonable enough, only it is just one more example of hiding, this time behind a very sophisticated argument. Certainly there were times when the environment at home was more conducive to bad behavior than good. Ultimately, however, I knew the difference between right and wrong, and at some level I made a choice to act out.

Do this long enough and it becomes a pattern, and the pattern becomes a habit. People start to believe you just lack self-control, or are a temperamental person, or that's just the way you are for whatever reason. If practiced long enough, we can even believe it really is not our fault. Blame shifting is just another form of hiding that prevents us from accepting responsibility. Did you know that studies have proved children learn to lie generally by the age of three without any provocation? It is the most fundamental self-protective behavior available to us at the earliest of ages. Running from failure is just lying to ourselves.

It is just as difficult to be on the receiving end of evil thoughts. Years ago a number of people came to my best friend and gave him a bad report about me. For various reasons these "friends" had kept a record of my bad behavior and now were interested in segregating me from my support system. In theory, this was purported to be a means of forcing me to see things their way.

When my best friend asked for specific reasons why these individuals were coming forward with this information, there was a lot of sidestepping. In response to natural questions regarding proof, various claims were made, and some were even put in writing. Fortunately, some of the claims were obviously fallacious and could be disregarded in the face of factual evidence to the contrary. Other rumors were not so easily dismissed. I had provided many people an opportunity to think the best or the worst of me. Which do you think most were predisposed to think, the best or the worst?

Was I really a scoundrel? Should my best friend side with my detractors? In the end my best friend chose to believe the best about me even though she was well aware of my shortcomings. I am grateful for her faithfulness and her truly biblical love. It took time for the facts to surface, and it would have been easy to give up on me. She chose instead to stand by me as a faithful friend even though her own reputation became a target. Her commitment to "think no evil" changed my world forever. So much so, I married her. Love thinks no evil.

Why is the opportunity to suppose the worst about someone so attractive? Why do we enjoy holding grudges? Actually, there is quite a lot of profit in keeping accounts—all for the wrong reasons.

Keeping account of the wrongs done to us is a subtle way of punishing other people. They have wronged us and we are going to make them pay directly or indirectly! It may be a withdrawal of support, a withholding of affection, or specific retaliation, and it comes from a desire to repay evil with evil.

In some ways our parents, teachers, or friends may have modeled this behavior for us over the years, and it has become part of acceptable behavior for us. Well, we need to understand that it is not acceptable. It is taking negative childhood lessons and turning them into poor adult behaviors and is not a very manly thing to do. We need to act our age.

Thinking evil of others often justifies our continuing anger that in turn absolves us of the responsibility to forgive. That is a very manly thing to do! Rather than feed the furnaces of bitterness and resentment, exercise the courage to release our anger and forgive those that seem to revel in thinking evil of us.

Holding a grudge is an easy way to gain control over people. It is a way of believing and insisting that they earn their way back into our lives. It is a way of manipulating certain guarantees from others as we passive-aggressively relate to them.

Tearing others down in our minds lets us be the victim. As victims we have certain rights, certain excuses, and certain opportunities to hide, and that is the crux of the problem. In the end, all of these strategies are self-protective, and none of them address what led to keeping score in the first place in a way that produces resolution or reconciliation. Paul had a great thought: "And be kind to one another, tenderhearted, forgiving one another, just as God in Christ forgave you" (Eph. 4:32).

He said this to a bunch of angry, bickering people who had difficulty getting past their differences. The tone of the words Paul carefully chose to use here (in other words, the impact if you were listening to this letter as it was read out loud) carries with it the sense of doing yourself and God a favor—get over it! The two thoughts implied are profound. First, do yourself a favor—the only ones we are hurting by keeping score are ourselves. Second, do God a favor—when has God ever asked you for a favor? He clearly has an interest in our getting along with one another.

I appreciate Rusty's unintentional contribution to my life. That experience helped remind me how easily keeping score for all the wrong reasons can sneak up on you and how destructive that can be. I appreciate my best friend's faith in me and how nurturing to my soul it was to experience the blessing of someone who refuses to keep score. As a result my inner world of thoughts and feelings is characterized by less turmoil, and my outer world is a much friendlier place for those who know me.

Chapter Eleven

Key 8: Does Not Rejoice in Iniquity

I got in a fight in boot camp. This big lug took a swing at me, connecting right on the end of my nose. Boy, did that smart! He was greeted by a string of profanities in response; and before I could get my licks in, the drill instructor stepped in. Standing at attention facing each other just inches apart in front of the platoon, the DI gave me a chance to settle things right then and there.

By now sanity had returned—I was literally staring at this guy's breastbone. I could not have picked a more one-sided battle. This marine was huge! Opting for better judgment, I declined the opportunity, only to be infuriated by this kid's smirk. I really wanted to wipe that condescending smile off his face.

Years later I ran into him in the shower. He didn't remember me, but I remembered him.

In the field there are no hot showers so you suspend a fifty-gallon drum above the ground, loop a copper tube through it, pour some kerosene in the bottom, light it, turn the water on, the water runs through the tubing, and viola, you have a hot shower! His shower had run cold, and he poured more kerosene in the drum not realizing the fire had not gone completely out. In the resulting explosion he was burned horribly.

I found myself surprised and ashamed that I was secretly happy at his misfortune. The score somehow had been evened.

There was a boss I once had who was really angry with me and deservedly so. I had screwed up pretty bad. However, his response was not only to discipline me but to go further to humiliate me, strip me of anything really meaningful at work, and generally treat me as an outcast. Years later I heard that he had been forced out of his role where I used to work for reasons similar to some of the criticism that had been leveled at me. I was secretly glad. Now he knew how it felt.

Once a public figure in Christian circles came to the institution where I worked for help with a personal failure. The ministry he worked for had remanded him to counseling to address the problem. I found him to be unrepentant and arrogant, just going through the numbers to avoid being canned. That this well-known person was giving Christians a bad name in the world because he chose to flout his position and privilege really irritated me.

Not too long afterward he was caught again and this time banished publicly. I felt justified, rejoicing that this counterfeit had been found out.

Then there was the guy who cut me off on the freeway. When I tooted my horn, he gave me the all-American single-digit salute and sped off. Not twenty minutes later I flew by the highway patrol car stopped behind his vehicle on the shoulder. In my rearview mirror I could see one officer slapping the cuffs on him while a second watched from a short distance with his hand on his holster. Good! He got what was coming.

The apostle Paul said that this attitude, rejoicing in iniquity, is wrong. It certainly does not love and reflects deeper problems that can be an obstacle to ever giving or receiving real love. Here is a literal way of reading Paul's instruction: Love does not find glee or be glad about injustice, harm, or wrong that may befall others. Whether the wrong suffered was deserved or undeserved, rejoicing in the failures of others is still wrong, still falling short of Christ's expectations for us.

"Hatred stirs up strife, but love covers all sins" (Prov. 10:12). "There is a way that seems right to a man, but its end is the way of death" (Prov. 14:12). Instead, we are expected to be more tolerant, understanding that finding some satisfaction in the trials of others may seem justified, but in the end it corrupts our capacity to love. "He who is slow to wrath has great understanding, But he who is impulsive exalts folly" (Prov. 14:29).

Sometimes my impulsive, secret response is to be happy about the misfortune of others—even though I know this is not right and don't want to be this way. One reason it is so easy is because it seems rational and appropriate.

In the case of the young marine, my sense of fairness had been offended because I didn't have an opportunity to defend myself and because the drill instructor chose not to deal with this cocky kid's attitude but instead exploited it to my discomfort. I wanted the playing field leveled. Ever felt like this?

The boss who took his disappointment out on me inappropriately (but not unjustifiably) left me in an uncomfortable paradox. I knew I was on the receiving end of the consequences of my actions, no problem there. However, his clear attempts to humiliate me and degrade me in front of others inflamed my sense of justice. I was left with feelings of anger I didn't know what to do with. I suspected the pot was calling the kettle black, and there was nothing to be done about it.

Later, when he experienced his own fall from favor, it seemed my frustration was vindicated, and it was easier to rationalize my own feelings about the situation. Sound familiar? Have you ever sought to justify your actions or rationalize your feelings in the face of personal failure?

Speaking of justifying yourself, that is exactly what I was doing with Mr. Public Christian. I was justifying the negative, stereotypical opinions I harbored toward hypocritical public Christian figures. I was coping with my embarrassment in a way that allowed me to separate myself from this individual in my mind and somehow believe I was better. Have you done that before?

The speeder offended my sense of courtesy and violated my right to safety on the highway. It is a good thing he was taken off the road, satisfying my sense of justice. Given enough ink, I can make my attitude in these events seem right. Only, they weren't—not according to Paul.

Do you see the pattern here? In each case it was all about me. I was the center of my universe, and when it is all about me, it cannot be about you. That is tragic because the only way I can love you exclusively is to let go of loving myself selfishly. In fact, all of the things Paul listed thus far are obstacles to loving others that we can only shed when we take ourselves out of the picture. Paul went on to give us insight into just how that can happen, but for the moment let's consider Jesus.

He was lied to and lied about. He was ignored, insulted and discredited, and attempts were made to humiliate him in front of others. He was tried for crimes he did not commit, tortured and beaten without cause, betrayed and abandoned by those closest to him. Finally, he died without a single word in his own defense or a bad word for his murderers.

Instead of calling in angelic reinforcements and rejoicing over the consternation of his foes as they got what they deserved, Jesus patiently suffered long, his love for us keeping him on the cross, paying the penalty for our rejection of God's own Son. "The Lord is not slack concerning His promise, as some count slackness, but is longsuffering toward us, not willing that any should perish but that all should come to repentance" (2 Pet. 3:9). "For God so loved the world that He gave His only begotten Son, that whoever believes in Him should not perish but have everlasting life" (John 3:16). To this very day Jesus does not rejoice in our sorrow or pain no matter what the cause. His exclusive love has changed the world forever.

Nowadays I remind myself just to let it go when the natural thing to do seems to be to get my hackles in a rise and look for ways to feel good about bad things that happen to others. This "get even" mentality isn't from God. Interestingly enough each person in these illustrations ended up living with the consequences of his own behavior—regardless of how I felt about them. My rotten attitude did nothing to change the situations or change their behavior. All it did was make me a smaller, less loving person. So if it serves no purpose, why not practice getting rid of it?

Each time I choose compassion instead of criticism, understanding instead of undermining, sorrow instead of sarcasm, or helping instead of harping, I change my world. Think of it! How would you feel if someone came to you sharing your sadness with compassion, understanding, and a helping hand? It would give me hope. It would change my world for that moment into a better place. It would mean you love me like Jesus does.

There are other implications tucked into what Paul said about rejoicing in iniquity as well. Buford was my foreman when I worked construction during breaks from school. Yes, that was his real name, and he was very proud of it. In the deep South names are important, and, as names go, his was a good one—especially since we changed it to "blow hard" when he got out of hand. Buford was always running his mouth about something, usually at several decibels above the threshold for pain if you were nearby. However, his reputation wasn't for being a loud mouth; it was for being a shark.

Whenever someone would do something wrong—bend a nail, have to make the same cut twice, wire it backwards, break a pane, whatever—Buford would get this light in his eyes like it was Christmas morning and all the presents under the tree were his. He would tear into whoever the hapless victim of a mistake was, cussing a blue streak, commenting on the individual's lineage, estimating their intelligence at less than moronic, comparing their abilities to that of a chimpanzee—all with a weird grin pasted under those bright eyes.

It didn't take long for us on his crew to figure out Buford delighted in chewing people out. It was almost recreation for him. Any opportunity to censure someone created enormous glee for this man. Taking such pleasure is also what Paul was talking about when he said love does not rejoice in iniquity. In this case the twisted joy does not come from the failure of others but from the opportunity to grind others down because of that failure.

Here is another twist. Richard always has a Robin Hood tale to tell in the break area. Yesterday it was about the fellow driving the supercharged Trans Am who got away from the highway patrol and even ditched their helicopter. Richard took great pleasure in lauding this driver's ability to elude the law. The day before it was about the housewife who put her husband in the hospital with a baseball bat to the brow when she found out he might have a girlfriend. Tomorrow it will probably be someone embezzling corporate money and giving it to the poor.

The problem is Richard's fascination with people who do wrong things and seemingly get away with it. He vicariously gets obvious enjoyment from the successful transgressions of others: happy they beat the system, got away with vigilante justice, or slipped one over on the corporate world. Finding pleasure in the success of wrongdoers is just as wrong as rejoicing in their failures or enjoying putting them down.

Proverbs 2:11–14 tells us that the way a man avoids this kind of pleasure is through discretion and understanding. "Discretion will preserve you; understanding will keep you, to deliver you from the way of evil, from the man who speaks perverse things, from those who leave the paths of uprightness to walk in the ways of darkness; who rejoice in doing evil, and delight in the perversity of the wicked." Richard doesn't think before he speaks and certainly doesn't have much insight into what his stories tell us about his thinking.

The concept of acting with discretion and understanding is one of thinking through how you are going to respond to someone else's failure. The word *discretion* as used here has the sense of a plan to it, something reasoned out in advance. The word *understanding* carries with it the idea of discerning between options, the right thing to say versus the wrong thing to say. It is actually a nice play on the words: *discretion* and *understanding* equate to planning and discernment.

There are some things we can think through now that will help us respond constructively when we are confronted by the failure of others. First, think through the difference between acceptance and approval. The adage, "Love the sinner; hate the sin," is difficult to accept for some people. Men especially can find this tough. So much of who we are is defined by what we do. A person who does bad things must be a bad person. Maybe yes, maybe no. The fact is we are never called to judge people in this way. We are told not to judge people at all (Matt. 7:1–5).

We cannot and should not approve of bad behavior. We can and should always accept the person. In fact, it is often this acceptance experienced by the one fallen that allows him to understand and receive our disapproval. When you know someone loves and supports you, it is a lot easier to take responsibility for your shortcomings than if you are struggling with his judgmental attitudes on top of everything else.

Second, we need to be committed to restoration and correction, not punishment. In relationships there is a difference between discipline or correction and punishment. Correction has in view making right what is wrong and helping to ensure that bad behavior doesn't happen again. Punishment only has in view inflicting deprivation and pain in order to get even.

Third, choose mercy whenever you can. This is always God's first reaction long before he gets to earthquakes and lightning strikes. Each failure brings with it a set of consequences. Mercy does not mean you necessarily remove consequences. Most of the time that is beyond our power any way.

Our dog Pumpkin had a mind of her own. One afternoon she refused to respond to a call to come in and ran rebelliously the other way, right into the path of an oncoming fire truck.

No one rushed into the street to beat the dog with a stick because she disobeyed. Obviously, the normal response in that situation is to rush to the dog's aid with comfort, healing, and protection. There will be plenty of time for obedience school later. How ready we are sometimes to beat one another up when we fail!

How would you prefer people treat you when you fail? What would help you more to accept responsibility and seek to make things right? A critical, judgmental spirit, rejection, and ostracism, a heaping on of condemnation, and calls for your punishment? Or an attitude of sorrow regarding your failure and acceptance for you personally, a clear commitment to your restoration and success, and merciful intervention?

Mercy in itself may be severe. Difficult and perhaps painful things may be required in your restoration. If the failure is personal and significant, some consequences may follow you for a lifetime. Better to make the journey in the company of loving support than in isolation, alone and despised.

Paul said a lot here. I can just see his audience chewing over these words and their implications as his letter to the Corinthians was read out loud in church. Love that is patient and kind does not rejoice when someone gets in trouble, doesn't enjoy beating him up for his problems, but also does not celebrate if he gets away with it. Paul did go on in the very next phrase to describe what we *can* rejoice over.

Chapter Twelve

⟫⟩⟨⟪

Intermission

We arrived, bent and nearly crippled from long hours in the back of a C-130 slung in webbed seating. We were lucky. Most came by ship, thoroughly green by the time they arrived. Put up for the night in temporary barracks, we were to be moved from Da Nang in the morning. Temporary was an understatement. These hootches had plywood floors, screen walls, sheet-metal roofs, and little else. The cots kept us off the floor but did nothing to relieve the heat or distract us from our introduction to combat.

Late that night the world exploded. All the greenhorns fled to an unfinished bunker lighted only by the explosions beating us down with repeated concussions. We huddled there, weapon-less, and wondering who was going to peer over the sandy edge of the hole we were in. Our trepidation was misplaced. Rockets had struck a transport aircraft filled with munitions at the end of the runway, setting off all the fireworks.

The next day we rode helicopters down to Tam Ky and ferried there to Chu Lai in Six-Byes. On the road outside the city sat an armored personnel carrier half in the ditch. Approaching from the rear you could see the blackened cavern just inside where the rear gangway used to be. As we moved left on the partially obstructed road, the rest of the story became clear. Dead center in the side of the vehicle was a perfectly round hole the size of a grapefruit neatly folded inward. The impact of the shell had pushed the APC into the ditch. The door was nowhere in sight. Whatever was inside had been instantaneously and terminally moved outside.

It struck me then, having been in-country less than twenty-four hours, how real and final combat is, how brutally it assaults the senses and offends your concept of safety and comfort. Incongruously, a thought popped into my head. I wondered, *Where is love?*

That thought did not occur to me again for more than a year. In between were many more nights of disturbed sleep and many more questions. At the time I was back on Okinawa standing in a missing man formation. Those of us who went over together rotated out together. The date was appointed before we left, and our experiences progressively branded that special day in our minds. So much so, that when we became short-timers it was customary to greet everyone you saw with how many days you had left. That was all the salutation you got, usually accompanied by a big grin.

The most hazardous time in your tour was the first ninety days and the last thirty. First because you were still learning the ropes, and novice mistakes could get you killed or worse. The last because the seasoned ones got the tough assignments because they were survivors and because they needed to pass on their experience to the novices—who could get you killed or worse. Short-timers tended to get cocky, too. Overconfidence and carelessness are just as dangerous as a novice.

Out of Da Nang we went in all different directions that first morning. Some flew, some were forward air controllers, others joined the ground pounders or went to different squadrons or maintenance outfits. We were replacements.

Now we were all standing again in the same spot on the parade ground where we had mustered for roll call before boarding the aircraft that started our journey what seemed like ten years ago. Now, as then, names were called in alphabetical order. To many there was no response. These had gone home early in bandages or bags.

My sons are marines, and both combat veterans of Iraq in the early days of the war. They tell me they don't do this anymore. Perhaps they should. There is marvelous closure afforded when, once again, you are reminded how real and final combat is. Standing there listening to silent answers to roll call, that thought came once again, echoing down the long brutal months: *Where is love?*

Vietnam for me was the start of a spiritual journey. Raised with a traditional church background, I had no clue what it meant to have a personal relationship with Jesus Christ. Because of a thirst to understand the whys of life, put there by the Holy Spirit, I was drawn on and eventually became a follower of Jesus Christ. However, my pilgrimage in understanding love has not been so well defined. Instead, it has been characterized by uncertain progress hampered by selfishness, self-protection, and self-doubt. I am still discovering answers that water my soul.

When did your journey begin? What questions are you still trying to answer? Do you even think about life, love, and what it all means?

My experiences as a young man brought me face-to-face with mankind's inadequacies and, even more important, my inadequacies as a human being. For me Romans 3:23 was a reality I saw and experienced every day, "For all have sinned and fall short of the glory of God."

Dramatic experiences tend to do that. In fact, when Paul wrote to the Corinthians, they were living in some pretty desperate times. He wrote to a church in conflict in a time when Christians were tossed out of their homes, out of the community, jailed, tortured, and murdered. Rome was a cruel and savage overseer. In the middle of this violence and drama, Paul talked about love and how real and final it can be.

Pursuing these two great questions—Who is Jesus? and Where is love?—has changed my world forever. It can change yours as well. It only takes deciding to do something about it. Paul took an intermission here, getting ready to switch gears. It is a good time for us to take stock.

Exclusive love motivated from a heart seeking the best for others is continually patient and kind. That was Paul's opening thought and one of the two pillars in our suspension bridge illustration. In getting us to the middle of the span, he listed things we need to quit doing: Love does not act out of self-protection, does not focus attention on self, is not arrogant, does not act improperly toward others, does not strive to achieve something for self, does not explode in temper tantrums, does not take into account the meanness or hateful acts of others, and does not secretly rejoice at the failure of others. Whew! That is a lot of stuff to quit doing. So much so, it almost seems unrealistic.

Paul knew our struggle well. "For what I am doing, I do not understand. For what I will to do, that I do not practice; but what I hate, that I do" (Rom. 7:15). Even when we want to knock it off, we find ourselves struggling to do what is right. However, I don't like the alternative of doing nothing. Giving in means I continue to live like a law unto myself—with all the consequences. It means I will continue to misjudge where freedom really lies and to pursue pleasure, or at least the absence of pain and loneliness. I won't care that I lose the person in this self-centered behavior and will continue to use philosophy, art, or anything else as an excuse for my lifestyle. Pleasure takes us away, and often it is pain that brings us back. What is your pain bringing you back to?

Paul listed some things that we can pour into our lives, replacing those things he just recommended we put off. When we stop certain behaviors or patterns of thought, they can come back easily to haunt us. They have become emotional or behavioral habits. We need to dehabituate. This is a fancy term for replacing one behavior with another, a kind of shortcut to getting rid of bad habits by replacing them with good habits so that you don't have to fight so hard to keep the bad habits from coming back. This is not contemporary pop psychology; it is a biblical principle.

Paul talked about being renewed in the spirit of your mind using just this technique.

> This I say, therefore, and testify in the Lord, that you should no longer walk as the rest of the Gentiles walk, in the futility of their mind, having their understanding darkened, being alienated from the life of God, because of the ignorance that is in them, because of the blindness of their heart; who, being past feeling, have

given themselves over to lewdness, to work all unclean-
ness with greediness. But you have not so learned Christ,
if indeed you have heard Him and have been taught by
Him, as the truth is in Jesus: that you put off, concerning
your former conduct, the old man which grows corrupt
according to the deceitful lusts, and be renewed in the
spirit of your mind, and that you put on the new man
which was created according to God, in true righteousness and holiness. Therefore, putting away lying, "Let
each one of you speak truth with his neighbor," for we
are members of one another. (Eph. 4:17–25)

Paul made a similar remark in Colossians 3:9 as well.

If you are serious about making a difference in your world
because you know better how to love and be loved, then follow
closely what Paul recommended in the remaining verses of our
passage in 1 Corinthians 13. Every time I find myself ready to
act in a way that I want to stop, I am going to replace that action
with what Paul recommended. I am going to break the cycle.
I am going to change my world.

Pray that God will continually get your attention to these
opportunities. God speaks through the Bible, gifted teachers,
godly friends and family, impressions or ideas inspired by the
Holy Spirit, as well as through pain and silence.

Sometimes what we hear is not God speaking. When it
may seem like God is trying to get your attention, ask yourself,
*Does it agree with the Bible? Does what I am hearing have the poten-
tial to make me more like Christ? Is this something my church family
would agree with? Is this consistent with how God has gifted me?
Am I convicted by these impressions* (condemnation comes from
the evil one while convincing or conviction comes from God)?
*Does the result of following these "messages" bring peace and health
into my life?*

Recognizing God's voice is not a complex or difficult thing. However, breaking bad habits may be difficult even when you may recognize at God's prompting that it is necessary to do so.

Those early years of my pilgrimage, questioning where love might be found, were not droll. There was even some comic relief. Willy-nilly is a good example of bad habits that are tough to break and a hilarious character to boot!

Corporal Willy was assigned to the defense platoon at the air base in Chu Lai, Vietnam. The defense platoon was sort of a ready reaction force whose mission was to respond to incursions inside our perimeter, and Corporal Willy was the driver for the platoon commander. Corporal Willy had a number of entertaining bad habits.

For one he was a compulsive eater. How a marine can get pudgy in a combat zone is beyond me! But there he was when I met him—an overweight marine in a combat zone. Willy had a habit of responding to the least bit of stress by eating. Considering where we were, that was most of the time. He was constantly canvassing for extra rations, trading for extra rations, even begging for extra rations.

Corporal Willy also had a habit of giggling under pressure, especially when everyone's anxiety was high. That, more than anything else, is probably what got him pulled off the line and placed in the defense platoon. You can't have someone giggling in the middle of the night when you are sneaking around, hopefully, undetected. Lest you think poorly of Corporal Willy, let me assure you that when the chips were down and the fight was on, Corporal Willy was an outstanding marine. He just had these bad habits.

Corporal Willy was also a compulsive avoider. The perimeter would often be tested. Small arms fire, mortars, rockets —all usually just harassing fire. In the command bunker, radios monitored the network as different positions reported activity. Often the defense platoon commander would want to take a ride out in his jeep to check the perimeter himself, prepared to pull the rest of the reinforced platoon into action if necessary. When the call came to saddle up, Willy-nilly was the first to complain, "Aw Captain, do we have to go? We can figure out if they need help just listening to the network!" Corporal Willy was no coward. He just didn't want to interrupt his nap unless it was for food.

The habit that earned him his nickname had to do with his startle response. Corporal Willy was also a sleeper. Anytime, anyplace, he would take a snooze. If he was startled, the normal reaction was to jump up and run willy-nilly around until his brain reached full consciousness and he determined where it was he really should be. Sometimes this happened even if he was awake and his buddies often took advantage, sneaking up behind him and suddenly shouting something dangerous just to set him off running willy-nilly around to everyone's great entertainment.

One night Willy-nilly decided it was too hot in the bunker to sleep and hauled his pudgy self and all his combat gear up onto the roof of the bunker and dozed off. His buddies conspired to get him good since sleeping on top of the bunker was a major no-no (too tempting a target). So they crept up real close and then in unison shouted, "Incoming!" Willy-nilly virtually levitated off the top of the bunker, leaped off, and ran away. We could hear him bouncing off the trees in a small copse behind the bunker. Everyone was in stitches!

Somehow he got himself turned around in the pitch-black and came charging back toward the bunker. The entrance to the bunker is a descending serpentine designed to protect the actual entrance from shrapnel from exploding ordnance that landed behind the bunker. As if led by magic, he navigated the steps down, left then right then left again turn and more steps down without running into anything. Then his luck ran out.

The helmet that would normally protect his head was still sitting on top of the bunker. So, when his head connected with the steel plate that served as the top of the doorjamb, he flipped over backward, unconscious before he hit the ground. That is when the laughter stopped. Everyone thought he was dead. It was also the beginning of helping Corporal Willy with his bad habits—once he regained consciousness.

Paul already listed some bad habits for us: Love does not act out of self-protection, does not focus attention on self, is not arrogant, does not act improperly toward others, does not strive to achieve something for themselves, does not explode in temper tantrums, does not take into account the meanness or hateful acts of others, and does not secretly rejoice at the failure of others. Pick one that resonates with you. This may be a bad habit for you simply because you have responded this way so often that it has become an automatic response. When someone approaches me regarding a bad habit, I don't want to run willy-nilly through the woods, nor do I want any consequence of my bad habits to knock me off my feet. I want to put off the old and put on the new.

Let's take acting out of self-protection for example. As a man I have a natural response in situations where I feel attacked, exposed, or vulnerable. I get angry. I get defensive. I usually attack back, at least verbally. The first step for me to take to break the habit of automatically responding this way is to understand why I find responding this way so compelling. In other words, what is the payoff for me?

There is always a payoff. For me, in this case, it is twofold. I build a wall of protection around myself, insulating myself from your remarks. I also retaliate, making it painful for you to continue the conversation. Nurture me, hurt you—does this sound familiar?

Now that I understand the payoff, I need to take a look at the trade-off. What am I giving up by behaving this way? I am giving up the opportunity to be corrected, to change something about myself for the better. I may be giving up some dimension of our relationship if I am successful enough in offending you, hurting your feelings, and driving you away.

The day came for me when I realized the payoff was not worth the trade-off. I had to make a choice. Acting out of self-protection was no longer automatic because I now knew what I was doing and had a choice every time I found myself in these situations not to do it. Repeated choices become a pattern, and a pattern, becomes a new habit, put on and replacing what has been put off. The whole reason I developed a bad habit in the first place was in response to a need. I need to be loved, not distanced from love by my own self-protective behaviors.

Sometimes I reflect and wonder if Corporal Willy ever outlived the "nilly" in his nickname, breaking those bad habits for which he was infamous. I climbed on an airplane and came home not long after that incident and never heard. But, like many cameos in tough times, the memories and the lessons live on.

Almost forty years later I still get a shot of adrenaline when I smell diesel fumes, aviation gasoline, wet canvas, cordite, or get startled by explosive noises. Though other experiences in life have long since become jaded and shed, the memories of those days are as fresh today as they were that day we stood together and remembered our comrades on that empty parade ground. Imbedded in those instinctive responses comes always the question, Where is love? I am grateful for these reminders that the journey is not over. In fact, when it comes to love, the pilgrimage has barely begun.

Chapter Thirteen

━━◆━━

Key 9: But Rejoices in the Truth

"Love does not rejoice in iniquity, but rejoices in the truth"
(1 Cor. 13:6). In sharp contrast to those that enjoy the
failure of others in some private fantasy, Paul described the
loving person as someone who congratulates those who accept
responsibility after having stumbled and choose to march on.
He is happy for them. Envy, jealousy, anger, competition, and
fear can produce in us a bitterness that keeps us emotionally
segregated from those who would otherwise be our friend
for life. We must learn to educate our passions instead of just
responding to our urges. Inevitably, our failure to rejoice makes
us the most alone of all.

One of the things that can keep joy far from us in relationships, even when we are not guilty of unloving behavior,
is loneliness. Just as bitterness can produce loneliness driving

people away, loneliness can produce a bitterness within us that has the same effect. When we can accept loneliness, we are at a place where we can genuinely rejoice with others even when the truth may be painful for us. Lonely people have the hardest time of all people being happy for others.

Terrance and Thomas are two brothers locked in a struggle for self-perceived supremacy. Terrance, the firstborn, enjoyed the favor of mom and dad growing up. A first-rate student and athlete, Terry grew up with the praise of parents and peers ringing in his ears. Tom always felt compelled to compete but was a different person from his brother. Tom's gifts didn't lay in academics or sports.

Eventually Tom grew jealous of his older brother and chose to pursue a more rebellious path, gaining as much notoriety in the family as Terry gained fame. As adults both men were lonely for different reasons. Terry never felt like he measured up, that there was always something else to accomplish in order to keep winning approval. Tom feared he would never measure up to his older brother, and his angry temperament kept most people at arm's length. Terry couldn't rejoice in the success of others because it meant, in his mind, they were succeeding possibly where he was not. When others fell into sin, he secretly viewed the circumstance as one less person in the race. Tom could never get behind someone else's victory over sin because he believed in his heart he was not victorious and that it was not his fault that he could not compete and win in the game of life.

Both grew up and married women who would not challenge their dysfunction. Both raised children who could not wait to escape from the home. Terry stayed true in a sterile marriage while Tom had numerous affairs and eventually divorced. Each was secretly (and occasionally publicly) critical of the other. Though they passed through life surrounded by people, they had no lasting friends and now were two lonely people unable to rejoice in the truth.

Using the phrase, "but rejoices in the truth," Paul talked specifically about a change in focus. Instead of being glad someone has failed, be glad when they accept responsibility and move on successfully. The grammatical contrast is strong between a secret pleasure about the problems of others and an inclusive and congratulatory attitude that encourages others to keep up the good work.

The word for "truth" used here carries with it the idea of embracing reality, what is true, with a positive attitude in a public rather than private manner. To do so builds a sense of relationship, a partnership in struggle, and community with others. Disengaging or being secretly critical disconnects us from others and compounds our sense of isolation.

None of us can escape the isolation of loneliness entirely. Loneliness is basic to the human condition. Normally experienced as a slight anxiety or fear of abandonment, loneliness can force us into community. In those relationships an appropriate intimacy can develop and resolve the feelings of loneliness as we enter into friendships that encourage, support, and guide.

Not belonging, not being understood, desiring a relationship with someone or some group that will not respond or cannot respond is a part of life. These normal experiences can motivate us to change and adapt and to restore or seek out healthy relationships, or they can make us overly sensitive to rejection cues and isolate us further as we withdraw from painful experiences.

Terry's search for appropriate intimacy with others eventually brought him face-to-face with Jesus Christ. When Terry found the Lord, his world changed forever. Graced with new perspective, Terry began the journey to finding the right place to ground his sense of self-worth and discovered new freedom to be the person God designed him to be. No longer a slave to the world's view of success, his attitudes changed and so did the nature of his relationships with his family.

The change did not go unnoticed by Tom. Yes, you probably can guess correctly that Tom's competitive nature pushed him into exploring religion as well. He and his family even joined a church for a while. But Tom did not find the Lord. Tom did find the bottom, though. Eventually he went into seclusion, estranged from friends and family. His sense of rejection, plus the anger and resentment he experienced, and self-pity ("it is not my fault"), left Tom depressed. Chronic loneliness set in.

Chronic loneliness is also a function of our developmental background, low self-esteem, personality, and the social alienation we experience. Social alienation happens when we believe we have a deficit related to expectations and leads to a subjective state of feelings. Our beliefs (mind), our motivation (will), and our feelings (emotion) produce withdrawal from all but the most conditional relationships ("you relate to me on my terms").

Terry found new ways of legitimately experiencing attachment. "For as he thinks in his heart, so is he" (Prov. 23:7). He became convinced that God's acceptance, and therefore his acceptance of others, is and should be unconditional. "I have loved you with an everlasting love" (Jer. 31:3). He made peace with his past. "If we say that we have no sin, we deceive ourselves. . . . If we confess our sins, He is faithful and just to forgive us our sins and to cleanse us from all unrighteousness" (1 John 1:8–9). Terry found new motivation to pursue a network of enabling relationships characterized by various appropriate levels of intimacy—sharing in common a new ability to encourage, support, and rejoice with others struggling just as he was.

I know Terry and spend time with him whenever I can. He is a friend unlike others, adhering to our relationship through thick and thin. Proverbs 18:24 says, "A man who has friends must himself be friendly, But there is a friend who sticks closer than a brother." Terry is indeed "closer than a brother." We have a better relationship than I have with my own brothers. Even when I have blown it, Terry is there: concerned, caring, compassionate, and a real fan when it comes to my moving on in the right way.

The phrase "sticks closer" is actually one word in Old Testament Hebrew. It speaks of the action of others to press themselves into our situation in a way that doesn't interfere but instead adheres them to us in a way that strengthens. It is a joining together like laminated wood that creates something new and better out of the combination. This is pictured for us clearly in Deuteronomy 4:4 where Moses used the same term to describe how the children of Israel were able to survive the wanderings in the wilderness for forty years: "But you who held fast to the LORD your God are alive today, every one of you."

I cannot imagine why anyone who can come alongside others in this way, rejoicing in the truth with them, would not have more friends than he could count. Loneliness for this kind of person will never be chronic.

Are you this kind of person? Perhaps you do not struggle as much or at all with the challenges Terry and Tom have faced. Perhaps the obstacles you face are subtler. Do any of the following resonate with you?

1. How I relate to you as a friend depends on who you are.
2. I am successful because I play my cards well.

3.   The potential for influencing others affects the decisions I make.

4.   I find I can change people to my way of thinking easily.

5.   When confronted I can become defensive or sarcastic.

6.   The information you get from me will be what I think you need to have.

7.   I am surprised when others tell me they feel confused or resentful around me.

8.   My boss is always negative and sometimes seems to sabotage my success.

These eight characteristics describe various styles of inter-acting with others. They also describe someone who is passive-aggressive in his relationships. This kind of person may not be self-aware when it comes to his ability, down deep in his heart, to rejoice in the truth and may be seen as friendly enough but somewhat an independent person or loner. Terry and Tom both entered adulthood in this way. Perhaps one of the reasons I like them both is because I did too.

Without Christ clinging first to our souls, laminating us into something brand-new, Terry and I would probably still be loners and lonely today. Without becoming new it is unlikely we would have ever developed a genuine capacity for loving others by simply rejoicing with them through our common struggles with failure.

"Therefore, if anyone is in Christ, he is a new creation; old things have passed away; behold, all things have become new" (2 Cor. 5:17). It is our stubborn refusal to be done with old things, old ways that keep us trapped in passive-aggressive behaviors and thus unable to rejoice with and for others. Here is an easy litmus test. Think of someone you have a relation-ship with, someone you would call a friend or better. When you need him to do something for you, would you characterize the way you interact or work together as one of persuasion or coercion? Passive-aggressive people live in a world of coercion.

The term *passive-aggressive* describes a distinct behavior. During World War II psychiatrists used the term to label uncooperative soldiers who consistently demonstrated hostility toward following orders. Their resentment was a mixture of passive resistance and grumbling cooperation. It has come to represent a pattern of negative attitudes and passive resistance to any demand for an improvement in conduct or performance in work situations or in interpersonal relationships. It is distinct and separate from any form of depression or dysthymia.

Here is how you can recognize it, guys. Your spouse says, "Yes, honey" in a way that immediately ticks you off. Then you get the silent treatment until you decide to let her have her way. You feel ignored and minimized. It is extraordinarily frustrating to have to deal with passive-aggressive people because their lips say one thing but their conduct is a different story. When we are passive-aggressive, we can use the old quip, "Nothing, I am just thinking," when someone asks us what's wrong. We can show up late to meetings on purpose. We can even read these descriptions of passive-aggressive behavior and decide we are not passive-aggressive.

Men do like to hide aggressive behavior behind an outward passivity. How can we rejoice in anything when we are so busy resisting, manipulating, and coercing others to come around to our way of doing things? If we persist in this kind of behavior long enough, it drives others away, at least emotionally, and we enter a lonely world indeed. Think about it from their perspective: If you always feel attacked in some subtle way but you never quite understand why, would you want to hang around someone like this?

Tom was like this. He pretty much grew up wanting things his way. Tom wasn't really a selfish kind of guy. He just wanted control and was a nice enough guy that he didn't act like a jerk trying to get it. Instead, he was passive-aggressive. Eventually in his career he reached a place of importance. However, Tom wanted a bigger piece of the pie. He felt he deserved a better title, profit sharing, ownership, and the ability to call the shots.

When he didn't get this, Tom began to feel unconsciously like a victim and began passive aggressively working toward forcing things to change. Not being aware we are acting this way is one of the big challenges with passive-aggressive behavior. When others fail, it just reinforces our passive-aggressive style. When others succeed, we are not able to enter into their success with any degree of happiness or support. We are unable to see the truth, embrace reality, or understand our loneliness is a direct result of an inappropriate need to control.

Tom eventually became so onerous to his employers they let him go. Over the next several years, he went through a series of less and less responsible jobs where he was either fired or chose to leave before he was fired. Now he is a maintenance man barely making ends meet.

Surprisingly, this is not an uncommon story but a too-common pattern among highly talented men that face life with an overtly passive-aggressive style of relating to the world. Tom's world is different now.

Colleagues, friends, family—life itself—did not come through for Tom on his terms. So he has withdrawn from life and prefers "to work for himself, enjoying the simple things and an uncomplicated lifestyle." Though he has stumbled and continues to march on, it is to the beat of his own drum in a world bereft of joy that otherwise could be his to experience.

Love rejoices in truth. There is no mirth in a falsehood no matter how closely held.

Terry, on the other hand, finds much to rejoice in. The idea of rejoicing is one of taking pleasure in something, finding happiness in a relationship, enjoyment in a circumstance, and satisfaction in the success of others. Somewhere along the way Terry discovered how to live without fear sufficiently to minimize control issues in his life and, therefore, limit the temptation to act out when things didn't go his way. Ultimately, fear is at the root of most passive-aggressive behaviors in men. Fear we don't measure up. Fear we are not in control. Fear we will be rejected for having been found inadequate in some respect. Fear we will never be loved.

If you feel isolated and alone and find yourself responding to people and circumstances in a passive-aggressive manner ask yourself, "What it is you may be protecting yourself from?" It can't be anything that God can't protect you from even better. Begin to choose to rejoice with others in their successes, particularly on the heels of their failures.

Paul used the word "rejoice" in the sense of cheerfulness. We are happy when others recover well from the sins that entangle them from time to time. There is an impersonal sense to the word as well. When others do well, we don't take it personally because we might not have done well in the same circumstances. It's all about choices.

I lost touch with Tom after moving away from the area, but I have stayed in touch with Terry. He continues to make good choices, choosing to love the way God designed us to love. Two brothers, living in two very different worlds. It's all about choices.

Chapter Fourteen

Key 10: Bears All Things

When I was in college I worked summers as an electrician on commercial construction projects. I learned a lot about construction that served me well in the years ahead as a manager for an apartment complex and later as a homeowner. Some of the simpler things about building construction fascinated me. Roofs, for example, were profound in their simplicity.

A roof provides protection in two ways. Most wood structures use tar paper or some equivalent to cover the entire surface of the roof in order to provide a moisture barrier. This is what provides the actual protection from the rain. The shingles or tiles that go on top of the tar paper actually are there to protect the moisture barrier from damage from beating rain, hail, snow and ice, wind, the baking sun—really, anything that threatens to destroy the integrity of the moisture barrier and the undergirding roof supports.

Providing protection, the roof endures the elements that would damage the household. What's more, the roof shields those within from the prying eyes of neighbors with a view, providing privacy. Protection and privacy that endures, that is the kind of love Paul was talking about in this phrase.

In Paul's day roofs were decks people used like a patio, or thatch coverings over the dwelling, or all sorts of construction in between those two basic designs. The idea of covering, protecting, and concealing, all with the sense of endurance that comes with a solid construction, is the heart of the word "bears" in this verse. Sometimes the word is translated *covers* because both ideas, covering or concealing and bearing up or enduring, are contained in the meaning. Love is like this, providing privacy and protection that lasts. Love is like a roof, profound in its simplicity and silence yet preserving those it reaches.

For us the assault is not from mother nature so much as it is from man's nature. Love that bears all things isn't just another way of saying we are asked to put up with a lot from those we love. Though true, this love is primarily directed outward toward others and is a shelter for them. That will certainly put us in the line of fire, but the intent was not our own protection in Paul's mind.

Gossip is one of the assaults we often have to bear. It is a loving act when you choose not to pass on a negative report about someone else. You become his roof, sheltering him from the embarrassment, guilt, or shame he may experience if this same negative report reached his ears. You may have to put up with the same attitudes or behavior that engendered the gossip in the first place and may even be ridiculed for the position you take. Love is your roof as well.

Often gossip is accidental or incidental to what is going on. Christians often have prayer meetings, prayer rallies, and prayer conferences that end up producing unintentional gossip. A word here, a bit of information there, someone puts two and two together, and gossip is born.

Mark and Jenny were leaders in a large church. They were struggling with their marriage, and Mark had done some stupid things. They were engaged with the counseling program in the church and getting real help. Then the ministry held a prayer conference designed to teach the fundamentals of prayer and give the participants practice praying. Mark and Jenny's situation came up, and, even though names were not mentioned, everyone knew who was being talked about.

People chose sides. Unsolicited advice was given. Rumors started and were fueled when Mark and Jenny refused, at their counselor's instructions, to provide any information to people outside their accountability groups. Their progress in counseling became difficult with so many other new and unnecessary issues to deal with. The whole thing spun out of control. Mark eventually had to leave the ministry, his credibility unfairly compromised. For the congregation, perception was 100 percent of reality.

On the other hand, Thalia is a success story. Thalia took early retirement with the hopes of enjoying her golden years in peace and relative comfort. But Thalia is married to an unemployed alcoholic who can be verbally and physically abusive. Her daughter is pregnant out of wedlock, and her son is in prison. In fact, a number of extended family members invade her home from time to time thinking she is the goose that laid the golden egg.

Thalia is also a follower of Jesus Christ and shares in common this faith with her neighbors, Bert and Christine. In fact, she often confides in Bert and Christine who pray for her and offer whatever support they can. Legal costs, demands of family and extended family, and poor decision-making on Thalia's part dried up the retirement funds. She lost her house and had to go back to work.

The neighbors were not completely ignorant about all of this, and their interest was piqued late one night when a half-dozen police cars roared into the neighborhood with sirens blazing, lights blinking, and armed officers surrounding the residence.

You can imagine the peppering Bert and Christine got the next day. What was going on? Is it true someone was shot? Did the daughter's boyfriend show up and try to take the baby again? Did one of the cousins really rape the daughter? Did the son break out of prison? Is this a crack house? Did she lose her money gambling? It was absolutely amazing what people were willing to think! Of course, no one ever asked Thalia. It is always easier to talk *about* someone than *to* someone.

Bert and Christine politely turned away all questions, assuring the neighbors that none of those assumptions were true. The neighbors, knowing Thalia confided regularly in Bert and his wife, did not give up easily. They were further assured that the proper help was being provided and were offered very appropriate suggestions as to how they could help support Thalia. Some chose to get involved without demanding details.

Others chose to chasten Bert and Christine (it was actually harder on Christine since Bert was at work all day) in the days ahead. Weren't they good neighbors? Why would you withhold information we may need for our safety? Secrets aren't good to keep between friends ... and so on. Bert and Christine's support of Thalia also exposed them to the dysfunction in the home, including misunderstanding of their motives by some of the family members.

Still they persisted in loving Thalia in this way. "'You shall love the LORD your God with all your heart, with all your soul, with all your strength, and with all your mind,' and 'your neighbor as yourself'" (Luke 10:27). In fulfilling this aspect of the Great Commandment, Bert and Christine were providing Thalia privacy and protection. They literally loved their neighbor.

A good bit of time passed before Thalia returned to the neighborhood and caught Bert going to the mailbox. She shared how well the family was doing. Her husband was off the booze and getting help. Her daughter had a job, had moved out, and was doing well. Her son was out of prison and working. The extended family had their extension cut off and were no longer a drain on her emotions or her pocketbook, and she enjoyed the job she had found for herself.

Mostly she wanted to thank Bert and Christine for their understanding and support. More important, for the way in which they sheltered her in a way that directed her toward the help she needed, strengthened her faith, and bought her time to take small steps toward healing free from neighborhood controversy. Dealing with unwanted scrutiny and criticism would have done her in; she was so fragile at the time. Love bears all things.

The next time you have the opportunity to be a good neighbor may not be in your neighborhood. It may be a colleague at work, a friend at church, a family member, or a total stranger. Here are some roofing guidelines to keep in mind:

If you come by some information that may be harmful if repeated, keep in mind that if you are not part of the problem or part of the solution, you need to keep a secret. Don't add to someone's crisis by passing on bad news.

Pray in private, not public settings about the people and the issues. Jesus, responding to the hypocrites seen praying aloud with great fanfare on the street, gave this admonition, "But you, when you pray, go into your room, and when you have shut your door, pray to your Father who is in the secret place" (Matt. 6:6). Jesus went on a few verses later to introduce the Lord's Prayer with these words, "In this manner, therefore, pray" (Matt. 6:9).

This word *pray,* so short in English, is actually a compound word with two meanings tied together to produce one thought. The first part means to turn toward. It pictures someone in a crowded place turning toward someone else to have a private word with him that others cannot overhear. The second part describes a personal conversation. Jesus was telling us that prayer is a private conversation with God. Good advice! Don't allow prayer even accidentally to become a conduit for criticism, judgmental attitudes, or gossip.

Respect the privacy of others. Don't inquire more than appropriate or necessary. Help them retain their dignity by gently turning people away that have trouble minding their own business.

Treat everything with the confidentiality it warrants. Assure others of your support, of God's love for them, and your commitment to them. What is shared with you stays with you if at all possible. You are their support, and they need to have confidence in your reliability.

There is a story about geese that has been around for some time. The author is unknown. Whoever he was, he understood how much we need one another and how much at times we depend upon one another to bear all things, cover all things:

The next time you see geese headed south for the winter flying along in that distinctive V formation, consider for a moment what is known about why they fly that way. As each bird flaps its wings, it creates uplift for the bird following. By flying in a V, the whole flock adds at least 71 percent greater flying range than if each bird flew on its own. We travel through life often on the uplift of another fellow traveler.

Whenever a goose falls out of formation, it immediately experiences the drag of trying to go it alone and tucks himself back into formation. If we had as much sense as a goose, we would stay in formation. There are times, though, when we all drop out. When the lead goose gets tired, he rotates back in the formation, and another goose leads. If we take turns helping one another out, fewer of us would drop out.

The geese honk from behind, encouraging those in front to keep up the good work! An encouraging word goes a long way. Sometimes bad things happen, and it seems we can't go on.

When a goose gets sick, injured, or just poops out and falls from the formation, two geese fall out of formation as well and follow him down to help and protect him. They stay with their neighbor until they are either able to fly or they die. Then they launch out on their own or with another formation to catch up with the group.

If we have the sense of a goose, we will stand by one another like that, bearing all things, covering all things, loving others in a way that will change their world forever just as it did for Thalia.

The word *bear* carries another related concept with it: the idea of supporting a burden in the sense of picking up and carrying something heavy. John the Baptist used the word referring to Jesus' shoes that he was not worthy to carry (Matt. 3:11). Luke used the word referring to the man carried in a litter to Jesus for healing (Luke 7:14) and again of the cost of discipleship (Luke 14:27). Paul used the word elsewhere connoting our responsibility to help carry one another's burdens (Gal. 6:2). This willingness to share the load is not qualified. It includes anything and everything and is not something entered into lightly by those willing to do so.

Bert is a load lifter in more ways than simply taking the heat from his neighbors about Thalia's situation. Bert is a medical doctor, and this serving and protecting dimension of his love for others extends well beyond the hospital. Through other friends of his wife, he heard of a man who needed a special medical test to determine the cause of periodic and mysterious internal bleeding. The insurance carrier wouldn't authorize the test, and this young family was going to have to forego the test or pay for it entirely out of their own pockets, something they could not afford to do.

Bert talked to the insurance company involved, researched the medical condition, and eventually satisfied the insurance company that the test indeed was necessary. They were able to have the test done immediately. Bert reached out and helped bear the burden of responsibility for arranging for this procedure for someone he didn't even know.

Another situation came to his attention regarding a woman suffering from a condition so painful that she had been hospitalized. Her husband was unable to stay with her in the room overnight because it was not a private room. Bert made arrangements for an immediate room change and went the next day to speak to the husband regarding his wife's condition and what good hands she was in. They were not Bert's patients and not even in Bert's hospital. He went as a friend to help the husband bear the uncertainty and anxiety associated with the worry about his wife's condition.

I have watched Bert sit patiently and listen actively to a couple unload their frustration about a dysfunctional parent, offering encouragement, empathizing with their situation. I know he gave a large anonymous gift to a friend who was unemployed to help him bear up under the financial pressure. He has mourned with another young couple I know who lost their first baby after three months pregnancy, sharing the burden of grief. He even makes house calls.

One of the couples in our small group at church has a young son who woke up one night with a high fever and vomiting. He went into a convulsion and briefly passed out. Mom panicked and called Bert. Bert could have told her to call the emergency number or even called it himself. He could have told her to take the boy immediately to the emergency room at the hospital less than five miles away. Instead Bert grabbed his bag and went immediately to the home—at 2:00 in the morning!

Because Bert was dressed in jeans and a T-shirt, the boy didn't recognize him as a doctor. He had only seen doctors in their offices or at the hospital, never in his home. He wouldn't let Bert touch him! Finally, Bert had to open his doctor's bag and let the boy plunder around a bit until he came up with a stethoscope before he would believe Bert was actually a doctor. Some people are harder to help than others.

This is true with Bert's parents for whom he and Christine are caretakers. They spend regular time with them, take them out shopping, for meals, and to church. They clean house for them and ensure the bills are paid. Bert and Christine are helping them bear the burden of old age with dignity. All this in addition to a family with five grandchildren to care for and a twelve-hour-a-day job with considerable responsibility for other people.

Helping others bear burdens the way Paul intended is not an occasional, once-in-a-while sort of thing. It is a lifestyle of choice. If we are strong for others only once in a while, there really is no sacrifice on our part. The idea of a roof over someone or helping to carry the load for someone is a continuous role. You are not just a roof for the moment or a wheelbarrow for the moment but a sustaining protector and load lifter people can count on. Bert loves others in a way that changes the world for them, and they can even be complete strangers.

In one sense this is God's call for all of us. Looking forward to Christ, the prophet Isaiah said this: "A man will be as a hiding place from the wind, And a cover from the tempest, As rivers of water in a dry place, As the shadow of a great rock in a weary land" (Isa. 32:2).

What a terrific description of love that bears all things!

Chapter Fifteen

Key 11: Believes All Things

Though the thrust of "bears" or "covers all things" is directed toward others and pictures how love becomes a refuge for them, the idea of putting up with a lot (indeed, virtually everything) without comment, criticism, or defensiveness is included. This attitude becomes the foundation for "believes all things." If we are to think the best of someone in the midst of difficult circumstances, we have to suspend judgment for a time and resist the temptation to believe the worst. We may have to put up with a lot.

Believe has the idea of taking something at face value, giving someone credit, thinking or accepting something as true, having confidence in someone, or having faith in them. Grammatically the word is positioned as a decision we intentionally make to treat someone with dignity and respect even if we know he does not deserve it. *All* grammatically refers to everything without exception. We cannot pick and choose what we will believe as the best or worst in a situation. Whatever that person has been involved in, said, or done we must believe in him or her for the best without condition.

Unfortunately it is easy for me to be conditional in my acceptance of others based upon my perceptions of their conduct. I am a man. I can be critical, judgmental, and even defensive if my involvement or responsibility for the problem is insinuated. Yes, women can be critical, judgmental, and defensive as well; but men have unique ways of expressing acceptance.

Some men are self-directed. That is, their energy, drive, motivation, and interests come mostly from within. Power and control are strong components of their interaction with the world. Acceptance of others easily becomes conditional on who that other person is, what he wants, and how he may impact my world. Often others experience this type of man as cold, aloof, and noncommunicative. Even when acceptance is not an issue for them, their silence and body language may leave others who do not know them well believing they have been rejected.

Some men are others directed. That is, their energy, drive, motivation, and interests are primarily found in the interactions and relationships they have with others. Fitting in, being a part, and making a difference are strong components of their interaction with the world. These men can get their feelings hurt, and you will never know it. It is easy for them to make acceptance conditional on whether or not you accept them. However, you will never see it—they want to fit in.

There are variations on self- and others-directed temperaments as well. Self-directed individuals could be skeptics or cynics. Combine that with control issues or overuse of authority, and you have a monster in the making. They will believe in you to a point; and then, boom, without apparent reason, they go off on you!

Others-directed men could be optimists or pessimists. Their glass is half full or half empty (and from your perspective the glass is empty). When reality catches up to them, they slink away. One minute they are by your side, and the next they are gone, and you had no clue their acceptance was that conditional.

Some men are risk takers, impulsive, happy-go-lucky, while others are compulsive, not easily rattled, and theoretical in their perspectives. Some are literal in their understanding; others are intrigued with metaphors and hyperbole. Some are dogmatic, aggressive, and touchy, while others are melancholy, plaintive, and self-absorbed. The variations are infinite! However, they all share a common capacity for conditional acceptance of others that can be masked and only revealed in surprising and often relationally damaging ways.

At the point I am no longer accepting of you, I stop believing in you; and because I am a man, you may never know my love was conditional until I disappoint you in some extraordinary and hurtful way. Because our temptation as men is to act this way does not mean there is no solution, that good character cannot prevail.

Let's return to Luke 10:27 for a moment: "'You shall love the LORD your God with all your heart, with all your soul, with all your strength, and with all your mind,' and 'your neighbor as yourself.'" Grammatically, "yourself" is positioned between loving God and loving your neighbor. Loving your neighbor presumes loving yourself first, "and your neighbor *as* yourself." This is not a narcissistic, self-indulgent love for self but an accurate appraisal of your worth in *God's* view. It is a healthy psychological outlook, confident self-assurance, realistically positive self-image, and maturely balanced self-esteem. It is a seasoned self-acceptance that enables you to receive God's love without condition and love others without condition.

When you can accept yourself, you are at a place spiritually and emotionally that enables you to choose to accept others. When you can accept others, you can believe in them. When you believe in them, you can love them. It seems to be a simple progression. In the real world it is deceptively difficult to live out largely because becoming self-aware, a key to change and maturity, is learned for the most part and not an innate talent. When we are preoccupied with self-acceptance, we are not at a place to be self-aware. We are constantly trying to justify, rationalize, avoid, and compensate for our deficits. In other words, we are focused on the fantasy we want and not the reality we live.

What I am today was a long time in formation. Genetics, childhood, education, socialization, and life experiences have shaped me; and the Holy Spirit has changed me. This is a profound experience that, like an iceberg, only reveals itself in small ways above the surface. Many of our attributes were formed in the womb and remain unchanged in their most fundamental nature. Other attributes have taken shape over the years, not really becoming coherent until about age thirty.

Some people would have considered me obnoxious in my twenties and thirties. In the Marine Corps I was a private going on general (that's a metaphor—I really was a private at one time and never was a general). I wasn't so much ambitious as I was interested in accomplishments that led to more authority and provided more money, which provided more perceived control over life circumstances. It was my way or the highway, quit whining and get with the program, lead or get out of my way, if you can't cut it—go away, keep up or get lost, and the best one of all: get out of sin, now!

I was insensitive, lacked transparency, avoided vulnerability, and used offense as the best defense. When I had trouble accepting responsibility, and being defensive or shifting blame didn't work, I went after the other person with a vengeance and was articulate enough to pretty much destroy the relationship. Fame and fortune were not alluring, but competence was. Competence was key to controlling my world. For men, it is all about controlling their world through whatever means their temperament naturally dictates.

When I was training as a counselor, my supervisor always used to always say, "All behavior has purpose!" It was almost a mantra with him. "Look at the behaviors," he would say, "their purpose may be inconsequential, but they have purpose nonetheless. You want to know what's going on below the waterline? Then look at the behaviors, all of them, consequential and inconsequential. They are like bread crumbs you can backtrack to the original condition." So, what was my original condition?

None of us are born perfect into this world, have perfect parents, a painless childhood, or failure-free lives. Every one of us carries baggage we struggle with to varying degrees throughout life. It begins with fundamental human needs for safety, security, and significance. We develop conscious and unconscious strategies for ensuring these needs are met and protecting whatever that is from being taken away from us. We pursue pleasure and avoid pain. Obviously, the best strategy is to have those needs met by legitimate, God-authored means.

In real life we can develop some pretty dysfunctional ways of substituting for God's best in our lives.

My strategies revolved around control of the people and circumstances in greatest proximity to me with the greatest ability to help or hurt me. My biggest need was to be assured of my value and worth, to know that I was loved, and to be convinced I made a difference to someone. My temperament dictated competence as the best tool for making this happen. So I excelled athletically and academically. I would compete in life until I won and then move on to the next accomplishment, next skill to master, next competition.

My goal was not more money or prestige. My goal was mastery of new knowledge and skills leading to greater competence and therefore more authority and more control of my environment.

What is your strength? In those behaviors you will find clues to your own strategies for creating self-acceptance. This is not about good/bad or right/wrong. We are what God has shaped us to be, and that giftedness expressed as strength is like a two-sided coin. God can use it for his purposes, or we can twist it for our own.

Your passive-aggressive behavior is a clear indication you have a problem with self-acceptance: If you tend to use sarcasm a lot, become defensive easily, feel like a martyr most of the time; If you gravitate towards people you believe can help you, believe most of your successes were exclusively due to your hard work, make decisions based upon potential for influencing others; If you find others responding to you with confusion, distrust, or resentment.

Hear what God has to say about you: "He raises the poor out of the dust, And lifts the needy out of the ash heap, That

He may seat him with princes—with the princes of His people" (Ps. 113:7-8). God loves us and will lift us out of our sorrow and take care of our getting ahead.

"The Lord is on my side; I will not fear. What can man do to me?" (Ps. 118:6). We do not need to manipulate our circumstances. God is on our side and will take care of all our needs.

"But the very hairs of your head are all numbered. Do not fear therefore; you are of more value than many sparrows" (Luke 12:7). God knows us intimately, the good, bad, and ugly, too, and ascribes great value and worth to each of us.

"Behold what manner of love the Father has bestowed on us, that we should be called children of God!" (1 John 3:1). We have been adopted into the family of God, warts and all!

"Since you were precious in My sight, you have been honored, And I have loved you; Therefore I will give men for you, And people for your life" (Isa. 43:4). God is willing to invest in us, so valuable are we to him.

"Being confident of this very thing, that He who has begun a good work in you will complete it until the day of Jesus Christ" (Phil. 1:6). God will continue to invest in us right up until we see Christ in person. Our value never fades. Our worth never diminishes.

Of course, the greatest investment God ever made in me was manifested in his Son Jesus Christ, crucified that I might have salvation if I so choose to know him. When I began to understand, experience, and accept by faith God's acceptance and belief in me, I began to accept and believe in myself. More important, my behaviors took on new purpose and began to finally and genuinely to accept and believe in others. Now I am free to trust God to use life's circumstances to meet my innermost needs instead of attempting to manipulate circumstances to satisfy my appetite for safety, security, and significance.

My world has forever been changed as result of his love in this simple manner. I am accepted. I have value. I can make a meaningful difference every time I love other people in this way—thinking the best of them, accepting them, believing in them, no matter what. The power of belief is extraordinary. What you believe in not only defines and shapes who you are; when other people know you believe in them, it can define and shape who they are.

I was six years old when I got my first baseball bat. Billy was ten. He showed me how to use the bat, patiently pitching balls my way, showing me how to choke up on the bat and step into the ball. He oiled my first glove and showed me how to tie it down around the ball to create a pocket. We played catch a lot. Our baseball diamond was pint-size, and the backstop consisted of chicken wire stretched between two stakes driven into the ground. I couldn't wait for Billy to get home from school to play baseball. We spent thousands of hours out there with the neighborhood kids charging around grain-sack bases and raising a cloud of dust every time we slid home even though we didn't need to. That's where I learned the game. I adored Billy.

I was a sophomore in high school when Billy disappeared. One day he was in college, and the next he was gone. No one knew where. There was a rumor he had gotten a girl pregnant and skipped town. Nearly a year later I ran into the girl he supposedly abandoned. They had never slept together, and she had never been pregnant with anyone's child. Not long afterward I learned that Billy had enlisted in the navy. I wrote him a letter and told him I missed our Saturday baseball games and hoped he was doing well. I didn't ask about what trouble may have

THE POWER OF A LOVING MAN

caused him to leave town but did tell him that I knew it wasn't the girl. I told him I believed in him and knew he would do the right thing.

We wrote infrequently. Years went by, and I had a chance to visit him and his wife. Billy decided to make a career out of the navy. He had married a nice gal he met at one of his duty stations overseas, and they had a son. We spent the afternoon and evening together, even threw the ball around in the yard. Billy confided in me that he and his wife were struggling in their relationship. I left the next morning, letting Billy know I knew he would do the right thing and that I believed in him.

A few more years went by, and I eventually heard through the grapevine that Billy's wife had left him. It wasn't uncommon in the post–Korean War era of the fifties and sixties for foreign nationals to marry U.S. serviceman as a means of getting to this country and then dumping them. At least that was the story I heard. Hardest of all, she had disappeared with the baby, and no one knew where they were. Billy was absolutely crushed. When I spent some time with Billy, we prayed together. He was going off the deep end, and I was concerned about his lifestyle. I told him I loved him like a brother and knew he would do the right thing.

More time went by, and Billy eventually remarried and had more children. We saw each other from time to time but didn't talk too much baseball. Billy was a very unhappy man. Retired from the navy, he just couldn't seem to settle down to what he wanted to do. One job followed another, the family moved every year or two, and then they just dropped off the face of the earth.

The only clue I had that he might want to stay hidden came when people began calling my phone number looking for Billy. How they got my number I don't know. They wouldn't identify themselves and were persistent in wanting to know Billy's whereabouts. At first I thought he was in trouble with the law, but law enforcement people know how to find folks and would have identified themselves in the first place. Perhaps it was creditors, but they know how to locate people as well and aren't sneaky about who they are and what they want. Someone was looking for Billy, and it wasn't because he had a winning lottery ticket.

Billy stayed out of sight. I heard at one point he was living in Florida, then in Illinois, then Nevada. A few attempts to locate him turned up dead ends, and more years went by. When his mother died, a friend of mine with contacts in law enforcement finally did locate Billy. The few days we spent together around the funeral were more time than we had spent together in a long time. I shared my faith with Billy, told him of God's love for him, and that I believed in him. Billy cried. He went on to share some of the struggles of recent years, and they certainly were bleak years. After the funeral Billy disappeared again.

More than a year later I got a call from him. His wife had tragically and unexpectedly died. He was alone again. His kids were scattered around the country, and not all of them were doing well either. Then there were more silent years.

When I am outdoors—especially at a ball game—and I can smell sunshine and sweat mingled with oiled leather and dust and, "Hey batta', batta'!" is ringing in my ears, I can still see Billy on the mound lobbing that hardball ever so gently for me to take a swing. When I would connect and the ball would dribble several feet, you would think I had hit a home run to hear Billy cheer! He believed in me, and it made a difference in my tiny little world—and I believed in him. I have believed in Billy for more than fifty years now.

Mystery upon mystery: I received an e-mail from Billy just a few weeks ago. He didn't explain how he got my e-mail address. He is doing fine, walking with God, reunited with his children, and back in touch with the world. Whatever ghosts from the past were chasing him he has set right.

When I asked what brought him back to the straight and narrow, he simply answered, "You believed in me."

Chapter Sixteen

Key 12: Hopes All Things

Most of us consider hope simply the expression of a wish or desire. "I hope you get over your cold soon." "He never gave up hope for a promotion." "She hopes to have the job finished by this afternoon." Wishful expectation, optimistic desire, grounds for feeling hopeful about the future: these all have a temporal quality about them. During an anticipated period of time, there is an outcome that has a chance of occurring. "I hope I win the lottery in tonight's drawing."

Hope remains something soft, squishy, ill defined, a reflection of our feeling that what is wanted will happen. There is an element of chance involved, hence the feeling part—we never quite have complete confidence that things will work out the way we want them to. Optimists tend to view the odds favorably and can have high hopes. Pessimists can be discouraged about the odds and not have much hope at all. When taken to the extreme, this concept of hope as wishful thinking explains why depression robs its victims of all hope, leaving them with deep feelings of hopelessness. When you can't count on anything it's downright discouraging!

The apostle Paul used the word differently here. Hope for Paul had a spiritual quality, not a temporal quality, and was therefore timeless. Since the object of our hope is always possible, always tangible, always there, and always obtainable, hope takes on the characteristic of a confident expectation of a future reality. What the odds are or how we may feel are no longer factors.

Hopelessness, however, is a learned helplessness. We are not born that way. For men this may begin with a mother who does everything for them. Overprotective and petrified of risks, their little boys are taught helplessness early. Their hope is in their provider and never in themselves. Or it may be the authoritarian father, strict in discipline and always demanding the boy to toe the line, stay within the boundaries, not be different—in effect, not take risks. Outside the boundaries you are helpless. A critical parent, always demeaning the boy, creates a man who can never get it right, do it well enough, or succeed to their satisfaction. Result: learned helplessness.

When I meet men who are without hope and yet otherwise appear to be healthy, well-adjusted, and capable, I know there is a parent, spouse, sibling, colleague, a someone or group of someones who have taught this man by their treatment of him that he is helpless. Hope for him will never be more than wishful thinking because others have sought to control him and rob him of his autonomy.

Buddy was a "good old boy" in the Southern sense of the word. We met when I was serving as a campus chaplain many years ago. Buddy would pretty much need reassurance about everything he was doing or thinking about doing. He grew up in a family that trained him to be helpless.

Constantly checking and double-checking, Buddy was driving his classmates nuts with his constant questions. Though he was an excellent engineering student with good grades, he seemed paralyzed by life and looked at the future from only the gloomiest perspectives. When asked why he was this way, Buddy would respond in his drawl, "I guess it's 'cause I am just a sorry fella."

When I met his father, I began to understand. Dad was a self-absorbed, insecure, demanding authoritarian who would never let anyone in his household outshine him. That included Buddy.

We began to work on Buddy's self-esteem and autonomy from a biblical perspective. With Buddy away from home for school, avoiding the negative influence of someone who must control the people and circumstances of his daily life just to feel good about himself was easy. Buddy began to take control of his own life and learn by experience that he was not helpless. One of the by-products of this spiritual process was the emergence of hope.

Buddy always doubted his salvation. This was true not so much from any interpretation of Scripture but from the perspective of his helplessness. When you are helpless, you are hopeless, and without hope Buddy had no confident expectation of the future reality of seeing his Savior face-to-face. The words of the apostle John took on new certainty, "And this is the testimony: that God has given us eternal life, and this life is in His Son. He who has the Son has life; he who does not have the Son of God does not have life. These things have I written to you who believe in the name of the

Son of God, that you may know that you have eternal life" (1 John 5:11–13).

God's promise did not change—only Buddy's perspective. Now he was able to grasp what was always there: hope. Job 17:15 speaks of hope robbers, "Where then is my hope? As for my hope, who can see it?" When a confidence in a future reality is shaken, it is traumatic: "Hope deferred makes the heart sick" (Prov. 13:12). Buddy became increasingly troubled after his visits home. It seemed like he was being robbed of hope. What was really happening was that his father, intimidated by his son's growing independence, was attacking Buddy's belief in God. There is no evidence so compelling that it cannot be disconfirmed by those who cannot afford to believe it.

So we went back to the basics. Biblical hope asks us to wait full of confidence for the result. This is the idea tied up in the word Paul likes to use when talking about hope. In Romans 8:24 Paul talks about the hope of heaven as a future reality not yet experienced that nevertheless is real and certain. In the Old Testament the root word for *hope* contains the picture of a secure place to flee to for refuge. Our hope does not depend on us, helpless or not; it depends on him. That is why the result is secure. That is why our hope is a confident expectation and not just wishful thinking.

It was not just Buddy's belief system that had to be shored up. His struggles were much greater than just being secure in his salvation and sure he was going to heaven. His whole life was wrapped up in feelings of worthlessness, helplessness, and therefore hopelessness. His very character needed a transformation. Maybe yours does, too. Paul's writings tell us how.

Therefore, having been justified by faith, we have peace with God through our Lord Jesus Christ, through whom also we have access by faith into this grace in which we stand, and rejoice in hope of the glory of God. And not only that, but we also glory in tribulations, knowing that tribulation produces perseverance; and perseverance, character; and character, hope. Now hope does not disappoint, because the love of God has been poured out in our hearts by the Holy Spirit who was given to us. (Rom. 5:1–5)

The message is simple and profound. Hope is based on experience.

Persevering through problems produces character. Established, proved character builds confidence. Confidence gives us hope. Hope, like faith, can be blind. However, God does not ask us to exercise blind faith. He does require us to step into the unknown—but based upon what is known about him, and his faithfulness to us. When problems come, we find our refuge in him, and that is where our hope lies. Not wishful thinking but a confident expectation of a future reality born out of experience.

God had to take Buddy through a number of life experiences that built endurance, transformed his character, and gave him a hopeful outlook on life. In order for that to happen, Buddy had to face reality, take responsibility for his problems regardless of where responsibility may lie, and take on his problems with the intention of doing something about them. It wasn't about Buddy's father. It wasn't about what happened to Buddy growing up. Placing blame just keeps us helpless. These situations were the opportunity Buddy needed to transform his character. When there is no opportunity, there is no requirement for persevering, for maturing character, or for hope.

"For we were saved in this hope, but hope that is seen is not hope; for why does one still hope for what he sees? But if we hope for what we do not see, we eagerly wait for it with perseverance" (Rom. 8:24–25). Without recognizing that he was an insecure, self-deprecating, and immature person and that he could be set free as a secure, self-appreciating, and mature man, Buddy would never have taken advantage of the opportunity to change and to be hopeful about his future. Recognizing the difference between what is and what can be is the opportunity—the gap—hope fills. That hope energized his efforts and drew him into a world he never anticipated—a world changed forever.

We have discovered three things about biblical hope:

1. Hope is a confident expectation of a future reality and not wishful thinking.
2. Hope is built over time as a result of character development, persevering through life experiences proving out the Word of God and not a function of personality traits.
3. Hope has no opportunity to be developed until recognition of the difference between what is and what could be occurs and is not simply a matter of deciding to have hope.

Now turn this around. "Hopes all things" is on Paul's list of things to put on if we are truly to love others. It is given equal importance to "bears all things," "believes all things," and "endures all things." How do we adopt the posture of "hopes all things" in loving others? These characteristics to "put on" have begun to have a pattern to them.

If we act as a shelter or roof for people and always believe the best about them, then it is reasonable that we would also always have a confident expectation that they can achieve that transformation in their character confronting them now. We can protect them, and buy them time, and act toward them with a confidence that they can persevere in victory. We are bearing all things, believing all things, and hoping all things with their interests in mind, not our own. Wow! Wouldn't you recognize love if someone treated you this way?

I was poor in math until I hit the eighth grade. For some now unfathomable reason, I found it easier to cheat and get failing grades than study and get passing grades. Whether it was burgeoning hormones or whatever is immaterial. Cheating is always inexcusable. My math teacher caught me cheating and had the grace to help me see the difference between what I was becoming and what I could be and came alongside with other helps that appropriately addressed self-esteem, learning skills, and socialization. I was pretty much an introvert in those days. He never told my parents. What he did was always exude optimism about my potential and the inevitability of becoming an A student. He created a space, a vacuum, into which dropped hope. I became as hopeful as he was.

He sheltered me from the ridicule of other students and the rejection of my parents, believed the best about my potential, helped make achievement possible, and had nothing but confident expectation in my ability to succeed. I did succeed. To this day I am the math whiz in the family. I never cheated again.

My world is a far different place now for more than just succeeding at junior high math. My world is different because in the eighth grade someone modeled for me what hope is when it is breathed into someone else's life. When I became a believer a decade later, this lesson took on new meaning.

Later, studying for the ministry, I came to understand more clearly this idea of biblical hope. Remembering my math teacher, I wondered if he was a Christian. Regardless, I am grateful for the lesson, for it has enabled me to love. Love hopes all things, and this hope is borne out in how we act toward those we love.

It was one thing to tell Billy I believed in him or to tell Buddy he could be confident in the future. It is quite another thing to demonstrate the meaning of those words by the way we act toward those we are hopeful for. My math teacher made it clear without using words that he had a vision for my life that he was confident I could live up to. He put his hope for the best into practice. When you believe the best about people and have confident expectations for their future, miracles can happen.

Here is a little hope-builder checklist to use in assessing how your conduct might instill a confident expectation of the future in someone else:

1. How often do you come alongside someone to offer assistance without having been asked first?
2. In your private assessment of the situation, do you picture this person as successful in the future?
3. In social settings do you often seek to draw out quiet or new people into the group?
4. When discussing future outcomes with colleagues at work, are you generally optimistic or pessimistic?
5. Do you remind your children often of great things ahead, or do you remind them more often of where they come up short?
6. Are you confident about your own future?
7. Do you congratulate others when they accomplish something noteworthy?
8. How often do you offer others a word of encouragement for no reason at all?
9. Do you thank others at work when they have helped you with something, letting them know they made a difference?

10. Would you characterize yourself as a wishful thinker or someone with confident expectations?

If you are an encourager, someone willing to come alongside and help without being asked, who typically sees the future in brighter lights than those you are helping, then you are a hope builder. If you focus on the successes of others more than their failures and can freely express gratitude for the help others may offer you, then you are a hope builder. If you can look at the future with confidence that it can be better than today without wishful thinking, then you are a hope builder. Hope builders change the world one Billy and one Buddy at a time, whether it takes fifty years or a single encounter.

The apostle John captured this idea of confidence in describing the hope that prayer gives us. "Now this is the confidence that we have in Him, that if we ask anything according to His will, He hears us. And if we know that He hears us, whatever we ask, we know that we have the petitions that we have asked of Him" (1 John 5:14–15). The reality that God answers prayer is not wishful thinking. It is a fact we can have confidence in. "Hopes all things" for those we love means making sure we are praying for them every day, capturing with confidence the best for them in what we trust God for in their lives.

Hoping the best for those we love is practical. We think about them in positive terms. We pray for them in positive terms. We act toward them in ways that encourage, lift up, and point them in the direction of a positive future. Love hopes all things.

Chapter Seventeen

◆

Key 13: Endures All Things

We had driven down the day before deep into the Rocky Mountains somewhere near the border of Colorado and New Mexico. The three of us had a number of things in common: former military, experienced woodsmen, and Christian brothers. This was a weeklong hunting trip in a new area, so the first day or two were set aside for scouting. We had never hunted here before, and the Fish and Game Rangers had told us elk were plentiful in the area. It was mid-October, and several snowfalls had already begun to blanket the area.

Our camp was in an old logging area on the top of a low, wide ridge above and on the south side of a valley, called a "park" in Colorado terminology. The park was bordered on the southwest by a high peak, on the northwest and northeast by two more grand peaks in the ten-thousand-feet-plus range.

A long razor-back ridge connected these heights, and all three peaks descended into the park through a series of gradually lowering hills and canyons to the floor below. The valley floor itself was roughly split in half by a meandering creek and groves of leafless aspens and evergreens. Otherwise, the park was open grazing with grass only covered in patches with the new snow.

The next morning we stood at the edge of camp scouring the park with binoculars, choosing the areas or zones we would individually scout. With about twenty-five square miles of ground to cover, we were going to have to split up if we had any chance of understanding how the game was moving in and out of the area. The morning was crystal-clear blue without a cloud in sight, warm with a light breeze coming out of the northwest. We had our weapons and gear ready to go, dressing in layers with the extra clothing stuffed in our backpacks for the moment. Of course, we had the ever-present orange everywhere.

The logging road continued from our camp down to the edge of the park, where we left the truck and got ready for the day's trekking. With compass and maps in hand, we marked the three zones each of us would be scouting on each of our maps. That way we would know where the others were if someone did not return to the truck at the appointed time and we had to go hunting them. This also was a safety precaution in case one of us got lucky and set up a kill shot. We did not want to be shooting back in the direction of one another. A rifle bullet carries a long, long way.

We set off in the direction of our chosen acreage. I moved west along the edge of the forest flowing down from the heights. The wind was to my right front, so I was coming from down wind. Nevertheless, I moved slowly, pausing often to check for tracks coming out of the woods toward the creek out of sight to my right and to listen to the woods and get a feeling for normal sounds—sounds that game moving through the area would change. When I reached the near end of my assigned area I turned right, crossed the park, and headed up to the ridgeline splitting the northwest and northeast peaks. I wanted to view the area with binoculars from on high to evaluate where I was most likely to find spoor.

Halfway up the ridge I crossed bear tracks—a big brute from the looks of things. Large tracks moving slowly but with purpose, no meandering and no pausing or stopping; this bear was going somewhere with a purpose. Probably a male based on size; but that was just a guess since there were no droppings to confirm the gender.

I got down on my hands and knees to sniff the tracks. No bear smell. That was good. I know what bear spoor smells like, and I know what a bear smells like from too many close encounters—something I did not look favorably on perhaps happening again.

The crushed snow in the bottom of tracks was already frozen solid, and needles from the surrounding evergreens had begun to fill the tracks in places driven by a light breeze. Just a guess again, but it seemed the bear probably started moving at first light, some two hours ago now, and was headed somewhere with a plan.

It was a little late for bears at this altitude to be up and about. This fellow probably was looking for just a little more padding before he cashed it in for the winter. A bear in the park would keep the game away; and, if he was looking for a high-cholesterol diet, the potato chips in our camp would make a great late-season snack, not to mention all the other foodstuffs. So, I reluctantly decided to see where this bear was going. I chambered a round, put the rifle on safe, and, holding it at the ready, began to finish the ascent to the ridgeline.

The top of the ridge was perhaps twelve feet wide with no brush or trees. This afforded a clear view down either side. I did not expect the bear to come up behind me without notice, but stopped every thirty yards or so to listen and pick out my line of retreat if he did. The bear evidently rambled without pause down the ridgeline like it was his own personal highway. After three-quarters of a mile, the tracks veered off the left side of the ridge and angled down out of site. The binoculars told the rest of the story. The tracks disappeared from sight over the top of the next ridge—out of the park and away from the camp.

I backtracked to the place where I mounted the ridge, surveyed my zone, and started down to scout the area. Once I finally reoriented myself to the area with the map, preparing to mark good still-hunting positions so that we could find them in the dark if we chose to hunt here tomorrow, I glanced back up at the recently vacated ridgeline.

Puffy white clouds were just beginning to appear over the top, apparently still some distance away. Mountain storms are famous for their ferocity and surprise, so I grabbed the binoculars hanging around my neck and checked the ridgeline more closely. Yes, wind was kicking up the powder and streaming it along and down the side toward me in thin almost transparent sheets. This storm was coming fast. Leading-edge winds were kicking up the snow, and much more was hidden behind the ridgeline than just a few puffy white clouds. I needed to find shelter fast.

I pulled out the map and picked a low hill just ahead that had the promise of some shelter on the lee side, away from the wind. Half a mile later I rounded the hill and found what I was looking for, a stand of trees—their boughs sweeping all the way to the ground. I marked the place on the map (who knows what the place will look like after the storm passes), walked into the grove two or three trees deep, and picked a likely tree not too tall to crawl up under. Though lightning is unusual with these storms, I did not want to be under the tallest tree. By now the wind was gusting stiffly, and the temperature had dropped a good twenty degrees. My layers were out of my backpack and on my back by now.

Removing the round from the rifle, I climbed up under the tree and cut a few of the inside branches out so that I could lean up against the trunk. The effect created was that of a cave. The thick branches all around me created cover all the way to the ground. The layered snow accumulated in earlier storms acted like a blanket keeping out the light but more importantly keeping out the snow that had already begun to fall and blow at face-blistering velocity. The surrounding trees would help cut the wind as well.

Though the ground around the base of the tree was dry, covered by the overhead branches like the inside of an Indian teepee, I still uncurled the closed-cell foam pad carried under my backpack. I used this to sit on so that the frozen ground wouldn't slowly drain my body heat. Though I had materials to make a small, safe fire, I really didn't need to. My multiple layers and boots kept me snug as a bug in a rug. I read my pocket New Testament for a while, ate an energy bar, and drank some water. Listening to the storm howl, I fell asleep. It was one of the most restful naps I can ever remember having.

Three hours later the storm was over. Like my friend the bear, I lumbered out of my momentary hibernation, reoriented myself with the map and compass, and headed back for the truck some five or so miles away. It was well before our appointed time, but we were not going to get any scouting done with two feet of new snow on the ground and drifts even higher, along with bone-chilling temperatures. A nice campfire and a hot cup of coffee, and we could discuss the afternoon's activities in relative comfort. Oh yes, we had a portable camping potty along as well.

The others thought the same way. As I approached the truck, I could see one of the men had already arrived; and not ten minutes after I hauled up in front, we spotted the third member of our party trudging across the park almost two miles away, his orange coat shining like a beacon.

While we were riding out the storm in comfort, a tragedy was unfolding in those same mountains. A number of other hunters, caught without the right clothing or equipment, became lost in the whiteout and froze to death. It took almost a week to recover some of the bodies from the covering of snow. The storm system moving through the mountains that day was one of the most vicious on record. We didn't hear about it until we were leaving the mountains days later and the incredulous reports were still being broadcast on the radio.

These able men were mentally and physically fit, no less capable of endurance than we were. It was not that they were unwilling or unable to endure but that they were not prepared to endure. Preparation is not just a matter of attitude but of practice. This is the sense of the word Paul used when he said "love endures all things." We are to be always prepared to stand firm under pressure, hold out, be firm and resolute, remain fixed in our perspective when life throws the unexpected our way. Love that endures is a practiced and prepared love seasoned by resolve and choice. Love often makes sudden demands of us, and preparation is everything.

Endures is constructed of two words captured by the phrase "under pressure." This pressure can come upon us in relationships with little advance notice as illustrated by two Johnnies.

Johnny One was the beau of a classmate of mine, Deborah. Deborah was an engineering student, part of my study group, and involved in the same campus ministry. We all knew Johnny One as Deborah's boyfriend. He was in a different curriculum and not involved in campus ministry. They married after graduation. Not long after, Deborah was diagnosed with cancer. Johnny One divorced her.

When those of us who knew them tried to find out why, the answer Johnny One gave was surprising. He did not blame hidden problems. He simply said he couldn't afford the medical costs and couldn't endure the pain. Deborah eventually recovered and went on to a full life. We lost track of Johnny One. I often wonder what else in life this seemingly capable, energetic, and intelligent young man was unprepared to endure.

Johnny Two I met later in life. A courageous individual, he had fought ignorance and apathy his entire career and was used to failure, disappointing rejections, and resistance to success. Virtually a founder of the concept of hospice, a widely accepted idea now but unproven and not trusted in earlier years, his ability to endure had been honed by preparation and practice through a love for others that focused on dealing with end-of-life issues with dignity. His wife, Betty, was also diagnosed with cancer. Johnny Two stood firm with Betty through it all as a living example of how love endures all things. Betty is now cancer free.

Johnny One was frozen out, caught in life's storms unprepared, unpracticed. Johnny Two chose to endure and survived the unexpected. Johnny Two chose an important distinction. Not only do we have to be prepared to endure; we must choose to endure; and in that choosing we must choose the right things.

Choosing the right things requires understanding the finer points of control: what we can legitimately control and what we should defer to the Holy Spirit's leadership to control. Galatians 5:16 and 18 say in part, "Walk in the Spirit, and you shall not fulfill the lust of the flesh . . . if you are led by the Spirit, you are not under the law." The word *walk* is active, expressing something we choose to do. We choose to act in ways—walk or conduct ourselves—that reflect God's spiritual influence in our lives. It is not something we are forced to do but something we choose voluntarily to do.

Led is passive, indicating something that happens to us. We voluntarily choose to submit ourselves to the leadership of the Holy Spirit. The Spirit leads; we follow. We don't control where the Spirit leads or what happens to us in the process. We do control how we respond and how we behave in those circumstances that result. Let me illustrate with another story.

My copilot and I were flying from Columbia, South Carolina, to Macon, Georgia. As we approached the Macon airport, a thunderstorm system unleashed its fury on the area. We were flying inside an elephant. Everywhere we looked it was dark gray without form or relief. No problem, we were on instruments and in radio contact with approach control. Then all the instruments went dead. On final approach at nine hundred feet with two twelve hundred-foot towers in the area between us and the runway, it was a bit disconcerting. My passenger, a former helicopter pilot, knew enough about aviation to start an icy sweat.

I began turning off systems, thinking we may have had an electrical failure and the possibility of a fire. The drill requires that you turn on the systems one at a time, allowing them to reset and hopefully identifying the system that took you down. One problem: it didn't work, and we were still flying blind.

The radio crackled to life, and I learned a once-in-a-million multiple lightning strike had taken out the municipal airport's navigational aids. The instruments weren't dead; they were just not receiving any signals. Other aircraft had been diverted or put in a holding pattern; but because we were on final approach and in potential jeopardy, we were left alone.

The air traffic controller informed me they had rudimentary radar capability and began to give instructions regarding altitude and bearing changes as he brought us in. I had several options at this point. Listening to the instructions, I could have considered it advice and simply chosen which instructions to follow and which instructions to ignore. "I like that one; I will do it!" Or, "No, I don't like that one. I'm not going to do it. Give me another one!" With this kind of attitude, I would have found the ground, all right, but by augering in, not landing safely. If we were to land safely, I needed to follow the controller's directions.

There was another option. I could have let go of the controls and told the air traffic controller I was fed up, and he was just going to have to get us down. That would have produced the same outcome, only quicker. To land safely I was going to have to accept responsibility for the situation, even though I had nothing to do with creating the problem, and follow the active leadership of the controller. This meant obedience was the only realistic option, not negotiating and not giving up.

Being led by the Holy Spirit is a lot like that. He leads; we follow. There is no negotiating.

We landed safely, popping out of the overcast right over the end of the runway. God has a sense of humor. When we had the runway in sight, the runway numbers were right under the nose of the airplane: runway one three. I left tire marks on the huge letters spelling out thirteen as we thumped down and rolled out.

Relationships are often messy things, not always smooth and storm free. Life isn't smooth and storm free. We can be asked in one form or another to put up with a lot, and these demands are often placed on us without warning. Now we are faced with a number of choices. How much do we endure? How long do we hold out? How can we best respond to the pressure? What do we dig our heels in over and what do we let slide? Is there a time to let it go? This is why it is important to understand, when it comes to love, what it means to be led by the Holy Spirit. The Holy Spirit will lead you into all truth (John 16:13).

If you are walking in Christ and looking to the Holy Spirit for guidance with a willingness to follow, you will choose the right things. Love that covers all things, believes all things, hopes all things, and—sustained by these—endures all things will change your world forever. That kind of endurance doesn't develop overnight. It is a result of many influences and experiences in your life contributing to your spiritual maturity.

The three hunters surviving the storm, Johnny Two standing by his life partner, the pilot landing the plane all have in common little choices they made along life's path that built stamina into their souls. Why do I tell these stories? Because life is not just a metaphor; it is a training ground. Love that endures takes a prepared, practiced maturity.

Chapter Eighteen

Love Never Fails

Interestingly enough, this phrase does not mean that love never quits or never comes to an end. Love dies for all sorts of reasons. People choose to stop loving for many reasons, good and bad. Sometimes love just fades away as relationships grow more distant, and, in the context of the true nature of that relationship, that may or may not be a good thing.

My first true love was a girl named Rebecca. We met in school when I was fourteen. I had a crush on her that lasted well past high school in spite of having other girlfriends. Eventually my infatuation developed into a serious concern for her best interests. That is about all the maturity I was capable of at the time. I was also shy and embarrassed about my feelings, and so my affections remained undeclared for a long time.

When the opportunity came to declare my puppy love, I did. Shortly thereafter, my immaturity caught up with me. I handled the long-distance relationship poorly, and we eventually called it quits by virtue of noncommunication. If I ever run into Rebecca, I owe her an apology for my self-protective behavior at her expense. Eventually, whatever love was in my heart faded away on its own.

Mary was a different case. As much as I was capable of in those tender years, I loved her and thought she loved me. That turned out not to be true in her case. Issues arose, and I determined in my heart to stop loving her, and we broke up. Years later I learned that she pretty much thought I was a jerk. I probably was. In fact, in retrospect, I am sure I was.

These first primitive experiences with love are instructional for me. Immorality was not an issue in either relationship. Fortunately, I grew up in a place and time that turned children's attention away naturally from such temptations. In one case love died on its own, and in the other love came to an end by choice. The fact that these experiences occurred at such an early stage in my life, uncomplicated by other dynamics that can make adult relationships truly messy, leaves them open for uncluttered evaluation.

I learned very early that love unattended can die on its own quite naturally and that love is a choice. You have the power to end it. In neither case did love fail. It just ended. Gratefully, I recognize that I was the operative person in those scenarios. Grateful in two respects: First, that my immaturity didn't emotionally cripple two people for life. Second, that it wasn't about failure. No one failed; we just moved on. That very first lesson contributed to my emotional health in a way that, combined with other learning, eventually led me to

Nancy. Have I told you about Nancy? She is the finest person I know, and she loves me, and her love never fails.

The idea that love can fade away or be dismissed applies to all sorts of relationships, not just romantic ones. More important, love that ends does not necessarily indicate failure. When the apostle Paul said that love never fails, he was not promising eventual fulfillment of our desires for a relationship either. It does not mean that if we love someone—a spouse, a parent, a child, a neighbor, a coworker (in the healthy sense of all those relationships)—in just the right way for long enough, that things will turn around or go our way.

Before we go on to discover what significant insight is locked up in this phrase, let's stop to consider for a moment where we are. Love never fails—this is the end of the passage in focus, the second of the two towers in the suspension bridge. The message of this passage is, "Love is patient and kind . . . and never fails." The grammatical construction that begins the passage is identical here at the end of this thought as well, marking the two towers, as it were. If we were reading these few short verses in the original language in which they were penned, it would start with something we would recognize as a signal, as if it were saying to us, "Hey! Pay attention! I am about to say something really, really important!"

The structure here at the end is the same. Love is patient and kind . . . (and this kind of love) . . . never fails! In between Paul described what patient and kind love that never fails looks like, both in terms of stuff we need to get rid of and stuff we need to practice, practice, practice.

Patience and kindness is characterized by a refusal to act out of self-interest or self-protection, is not arrogant and does not act improperly, does not put self above others, explode in temper tantrums, take into account the weakness or meanness of others, and does not rejoice in the failure of others.

On the contrary, patient and kind love rejoices in the success and growth of others, acts to protect others, has confidence in others, always has the highest expectations, and stands up under pressure to be less loving. That's why it never fails. So what does failure mean in this context?

The apostle Paul chose to use a word here for *fail* that is infrequently used in the New Testament. It has a unique sense to it. Born of two even older ideas, there is a double meaning.

The first idea captures the picture of an ancient mariner, a navigator, constantly checking his course and making sure the ship is not driven off course by the tossing waves, sea currents, or wind. Paul used this idea (but not the same words) in 1 Corinthians 15:58 when he said, "Therefore, my beloved brethren, be steadfast, immovable, always abounding in the work of the Lord, knowing that your labor is not in vain in the Lord." That is the idea—steadfast and immovable—nothing distracts you, interrupts you, or causes you to lose sight of the purpose or goal.

The second idea focuses on the impact of this kind of love. It never produces harm or destruction. Relationships characterized by Paul's idea of love in this sense are not toxic and do not leave emotionally or physically injured people in its wake. The effect is encouraging, nurturing, and positive. No one gets disposed of, marginalized, or made to feel they somehow have less value.

Where does the popular idea come from that this phrase means love never comes to an end? When you put these two ideas together—that love is never driven off course and never causes harm—you have the picture of love that is not ineffectual, that hangs in there and perseveres. It does not cease, fall down, or fall away—other paraphrases of this word as used in 1 Corinthians 13:8. Paul used a related word in Romans 9:6 when he said, "But it is not that the Word of God has taken no effect," pointing out that the effect of the Word continues whether we respond to it or not. The effect of this kind of love does not come to an end even though we may or may not continue to be recipients. The emphasis is on the effectual quality of love that is patient and kind.

Gunny Baker knew how to love this way. The incongruity of the circumstances in which I served with Gunny Baker in Vietnam highlights yet another lesson for me about love. Gunnery sergeants in the Marine Corps are gods to the enlisted men under their command. Older, wiser, tougher, these non-commissioned officers wield tremendous power over the lives of the young men under their command. Most were just out of high school and had left their Rebeccas and Marys behind for what they thought was high adventure and, in reality, turned out to be a test of their mortality.

Some of these young men had gotten into trouble with the law, and the Marine Corps was the alternative to jail they had been offered. Some came from economic circumstances that deprived them of even a high school education. Some were just rotten kids. Gunny always asked for all the hard cases and, for as long as I knew him, turned these boys into good men. He wasn't a pushover. Tough as nails, he set clear standards and even clearer consequences if you didn't live up to them.

He had an odd talent. Gunny could hurl anything—a screwdriver, a hammer, a knife, an axe, and even a shovel—from outrageous distances and embed them in whatever target had been chosen. His "kids," as we called them, would run around picking unlikely objects of dirt, rock, wood, and steel for him to impale, taking bets whether or not he would succeed. His other talent was a patient kindness, out of place in a combat zone, with each young man.

When not in the field or on duty, he taught them basic electricity, refrigeration, plumbing, and carpentry. Somehow, I never knew how, he would arrange for jobs back in the States for these young men when they finished their tours of duty. Keeping in touch, he made sure they continued their training until they became journeymen or obtained their trade license.

When they screwed up, he didn't shield them from punishment but appeared with them before the commanding officer to balance the charge with a description of the young offender's good qualities and educational progress. Punishment often meant mess duty, garbage detail, latrines or some other unpleasant period of extra duty. Gunny always came by to see how his boys were doing, offering encouraging words or bringing by C rations because they had missed chow call.

They always had to write home, and Gunny mailed the letters. When the Chaplain was around to hold services, there was Gunny up front with all the kids—eyes front and you better pay attention! He worked through tough personal and family issues with them and taught them how to think and act in ways that not only protected their lives but also gave them a maturing hope for the future away from this place. When we lost anyone, Gunny took it like he lost a son.

Gunny wasn't like that with just the kids. He was like that with everyone, always consistent, never changing. Some did not respond to him at all and chose their own path. Even though they separated themselves from the influence of this patient, kind man, however, it did not change how he acted toward them. His love never flagged or failed whether anyone received or rejected his instruction and help.

He was instrumental in setting up a radio link that everyone, enlisted and officer alike, could use to call home. The field radio was patched into another more powerful radio that was in turn in touch with a ham operator. The HF setup was patched into the phone system in Hawaii, and Ma Bell was kind enough to place calls at no charge. The only trick was to get used to the delay caused by all the links and the one-way communication that allowed only one person to talk at a time followed by "over" to signal you were ready to hear the reply. These days that kind of thing is commonplace. Back in 1968, it was miraculous!

I will always remember one particular day in 1968. We had been absolutely hammered over the last twelve hours when Gunny showed up at my bunker early in the morning. It was, we were to learn, the Tet Offensive; and things were so tough we couldn't even get our aircraft airborne.

My appointed time to make my call home had arrived. Afraid I would miss my window of opportunity, he had risked his life to find me and get me to the field radio. It was like a moment out of time. There I was, in the middle of a war that at the moment seemed to be quite personal, talking to my mother as she sat at her table eating breakfast and drinking coffee half a world away.

Gunny stood behind me as I hunched down over the radio trying to get Mom to slow down and understand she had to say "over" and stop talking so I could get a word in edgewise. He had his weapon drawn just in case we were interrupted. Looking at him and listening to Mom, I had one of those freaky out-of-body moments. Suddenly, the world was quiet, and I was observing the whole scene in my mind's eye.

Then it came to me—the lesson. This guy never quits. He may change course for good reasons, but even then his love is directed somewhere else. From my perspective love may fade away or intentionally end, but from his perspective his love for others remained unaffected. It was a constant. It never failed.

Love that never fails is always about us and never about the other person. Whether it is right to direct our attention somewhere else or not, we are always to love without fail. Those who fall under the umbrella of that commitment in our lives will never experience harm or destruction from us.

Gunny's love for his fellowman was so disconnected and antithetical to what we were doing at the moment that it shone like a beacon in the night. I still respond to that memory whenever I think about giving up on somebody.

Gunny Baker and I parted ways just a few months later. I saw him once back in the States just before he retired. I wonder how many young lives he changed for the better over his twenty-two-year career.

Who have you given up on? Was that the right change of course for you? I have learned to always ask those questions.

Jesus is good example of love that never is drawn off course, never causes harm, never ceases or fails. Jesus said, "Take my yoke upon you and learn from Me, for I am gentle and lowly in heart, and you will find rest for your souls. For My yoke is easy and My burden is light" (Matt. 11:29–30). Scholars differ in which kind of yoke is meant here. The more common view is that this is the yoke worn by a pair of oxen working. In this view Jesus shares the yoke with us, making the burden light. A less-known view is that this is a personal yoke of the kind used by individuals to carry water, loads to the market, or while working. The yoke is carved for the fit and comfort of the yoke's owner, and a borrowed yoke is inevitably uncomfortable. The point is that Jesus' yoke always fits perfectly.

In either case, the metaphor works. Embraced by the love of Christ, we will experience no distraction, no harm under his yoke. He says his eye is always upon us (Ps. 33:18), and in Hebrews 13:5 Jesus said, "I will never leave you nor forsake you." We find ourselves constantly under the umbrella of his unfailing love. When we experience love like this through the Christlike commitment of others to us, our world is changed forever.

I work in a hospital. I see patients and their visitors every day. They are all in some sort of physical or mental state of concern, worry, pain, or fear. I see physicians and employees harried by the constant press of the needs of those they serve and often hobbled by the expectation they can work miracles while knowing they cannot.

Health care is a tough profession, and acute care hospitals just magnify and compress the pressures. There are opportunities every moment to be patient, kind, and consistent in love directed toward others, even strangers. The reality that many times a word of comfort or support meets with anger, or an act of helpfulness goes unnoticed without so much as a thank you, does not mean it has not accomplished something good.

This is where I start practicing love every day—right in the middle of life in all its imperfections. I expect to see people at their worst. What has brought them here is not usually the best of circumstances. I often also see people at their best, giving life, and hope, and love. I see them changing someone's world every single day because their love never fails.

What about your world, are you satisfied with it? You can do something about it. You can change your world a little bit every day. It's really a very manly pursuit, being a world changer. It just takes a little love. No one would ever accuse

Gunny Baker of being unmanly. Nor would they accuse him of being unloving. A good man finds no contradiction in being loving. Many good men, however, find themselves unable to love even when that is the earnest desire of their hearts. They just are not healthy enough to love. That was another lesson about love that I had ahead of me. Healthy loves best.

Chapter Nineteen

Healthy Loves Best

We have all heard the saying: eat right, exercise, and get plenty of rest. Probably we have heard it so often we don't even pay attention anymore. Yet this simple adage contains enormous wisdom. How we may be doing in one area of our health deeply impacts another. Out of shape? Overweight? You may be a candidate for depression or diabetes. Tired all the time? You may have difficulty trusting others, even God. As the psalmist said, we are indeed fearfully and wonderfully made (Ps. 139:13–16). Adam is a case in point.

Adam grew up with two siblings in a home replete with mom and dad and a white picket fence. Both his parents worked and when they were home seemed to spend most of their time criticizing each other and yelling at the kids. Dad drank and was probably a functional alcoholic. Though the kids were never physically abused, there was plenty of emotional or psychological abuse to go around. Neither parent was generous with praise or outright expressions of love for the kids. Oh, they knew they were loved—it just was not expressed openly that often.

Without the money or grades to get him into college, Adam joined the army after high school on a college assistance program. During his four years, which stretched to six, he met and married his wife and had two children (partly why his tour stretched to six years). His wife was a good enough person. She certainly loved him, but her glass was always half empty. Because Adam had grown up with conflict and criticism, his wife's nagging, critical spirit just seemed normal—actually, only half as bad since he grew up with two critical parents constantly pointing out where he failed to measure up.

When Adam completed his military service, he cashed in on his educational allowance and attended a trade school full-time. The two-year program was going to turn him out as a licensed electrician. In order to make ends meet, Adam also worked two part-time jobs in the evenings and on weekends. Upon graduation Adam was hired by a commercial construction company and began his career.

Both churchgoing Christians, Adam and his wife had faithfully attended church with their family during these years. In fact, they had become deeply involved as lay workers in their church. With a growing heart for ministry, Adam exchanged the time invested in two part-time jobs when he was in school for night school at the local Bible college and weekends packed with ministry activities. Life seemed to be working out for this young family. Two kids, a mom and a dad, and a home with a white picket fence. Successful in his job (he was a foreman now), involved in the community, and continuing to improve himself—you would think it was the ideal life story.

When I met Adam, he was totally stressed out, chronically fatigued, and mildly depressed, though he denied the latter. Unable to concentrate for long on anything, skeptical, distrustful, having problems with short-term memory, and always busy, Adam was disthymic.

Disthymia is a low-grade, almost unnoticeable depression that takes years to develop, usually brought on by a long series of negative life events or conditions. Judging others negatively, slight paranoia, blame fixing, avoidance, and denial are all part of the package but never so visible as to be diagnosable.

One clue to Adam's condition was his feelings. If he felt emotion to any strong degree at all, it was always and only anger—and anger was easily and quickly displayed. Brought on by too many years of little exercise, a cup of coffee for breakfast on the way out the door, and junk food all day long in a stress-filled life, Adam also had type 2 diabetes.

Emotionally and physically Adam was a wreck. Spiritually, he was in a wasteland. Angry at God for trapping him in a relationship with a woman he no longer felt he loved, frustrated with teenagers who couldn't seem to stay out of trouble at school, and feeling trapped by it all, Adam would just sit and stew in church. He no longer read his Bible, prayed, or enjoyed his time with other believers. His schoolwork was falling behind, and he really didn't care anymore. Adam was no longer healthy enough on any plane to love anymore. How did he get to this place?

Adam is—and was—codependent. All of his physical, emotional, and spiritual woes are just symptoms. The cause lies in the living of his life built upon a poor foundation. Let's back up and see how all this came together to produce such sadness, anger, and hopelessness.

God has designed into each of us wonderful self-regulating and self-protecting mechanisms. The autonomic nervous system is one of these. Whenever our bodies are challenged by almost anything that happens to us, the autonomic nervous system stimulates the output of cortisol and adrenalin. This could be a result of getting out of bed, walking up the driveway from the mailbox, teaching Sunday school in church, or getting yelled at by the boss. The adrenalin keeps us alert by increasing our blood pressure and making the heart beat faster, while cortisol acts to stimulate the replenishment of energy as well as helping us to remember important things and kicking our immune system into readiness in order to handle infection or injury.

When we are subject to chronic stress, we can pay a price of too much of a good thing. Overactivity of the autonomic nervous system can produce elevated levels of sugar in the blood. Inadequate sleep adds to the effect, and over time insulin levels rise. Insulin is the chemical manufactured in the pancreas to control blood sugar. Without proper diet and rest, and with our bodies reacting every time we are stressed out, we have left the door open to type 2 diabetes, high blood pressure, and heart disease.

Given enough time, other brain structures housing short-term memory are affected, and we can lose verbal and spatial memory—one reason why traumatic memories are not right at our fingertips. Eventually even the immune system becomes impaired, and simple colds or infections take forever to get over. Reaching for a cigarette or a drink every time we are stressed out instead of heading for the gym just makes it worse.

The autonomic nervous system regulates muscles and glands and helps regulate the heart, stomach, and intestines. It is where our fight-or-flight response to crisis occurs. In crisis

THE POWER OF A LOVING MAN

our pupils may dilate, our mouth goes dry, heart rate increases, breathing may become difficult, our stomach becomes upset, we may become constipated—all of these are evidence of the autonomic nervous system working. All of this affects the hypothalamus. The job of the hypothalamus is to maintain the body's status quo. When the body sends signals that all is not right, the hypothalamus, among other things, kicks the endocrine system into high gear.

Are you getting the picture that everything seems connected to everything else? The effects of an angry conversation, bitterness, fatigue, disappointment, fear, loneliness, or hurt feelings don't just disappear into thin air. They have an impact and, if repeated often and seriously enough, a lasting impact.

The endocrine system is key in regulating mood, growth and development, metabolism, and sexual function. Are you moody, depressed? Are you gaining weight unexpectedly? Has your sex drive disappeared? There are many causes of these symptoms. However, these may be due to changes in your endocrine system. The foundations of the endocrine system are the hormones and glands that regulate many of our bodily functions.

So interconnected are these basic functions that Adam's body chemistry affected his thinking, while at the same time Adam's thinking affected his body chemistry, and it all came crashing down.

Then there is the hippocampus. Emotion and memory are closely related. The limbic system is responsible for transforming information into memory. The main location for this transfer is the hippocampus. When the body is constantly in a fight-or-flight status, the hippocampus tends to shut down, and new memories form with difficulty. In cases of severe depression, this organ can actually shrink.

Adam's childhood memories were few and confused. Though he would not characterize growing up as tough, he had few memories earlier than age six to confirm or disaffirm this feeling. When Adam finally sought medical help, he was referred to a Christian psychiatrist. One of the first things the psychiatrist required was a full physical just to determine what Adam's body was doing or not doing. The question eventually came into focus, "Where is all the energy coming from that is driving these maladies?" That is when codependency became part of the equation.

Codependency is a learned behavior. That means it can be unlearned. It is an emotional and behavioral response to life that impairs one's ability to have healthy relationships. Codependent people often maintain relationships that are one-sided and emotionally destructive or abusive. For Adam this behavior was learned in childhood, responding to the animosity openly displayed between his parents and often directed toward him and his siblings. At first, "codependence" was a label applied to relationships in families of alcoholics. It is a behavior learned by watching other family members who display this kind of behavior.

Persons in a relationship with an addicted person, regardless of the addiction, as well as those living with the chronically physically or mentally ill were later added to the classification of codependence. It has been learned since that codependent behavior can develop as a coping mechanism in any dysfunctional family and is passed on from one generation to the next.

A dysfunctional family is any family in which members experience fear, anger, pain, or shame that is ignored or denied. Addiction to drugs, alcohol, relationships, work, food, sex, or gambling can set the stage for codependent development. Physical, emotional, or sexual abuse is involved. Adam had grown up in a household that used shaming to manipulate behaviors, and his marriage continued the pattern of emotional abuse in the form of constant criticism. He had also learned how to be a survivor.

Dysfunctional families do not talk about the problems that exist. Adam learned to avoid confrontation, repress his emotions, and disregard his own needs, burying himself in busyness and a need to continually excel in order to avoid the pain. His behaviors helped him to deny, ignore, or avoid difficult emotions. This contributed to his wife's growing feeling of isolation, and many of her behaviors were poorly chosen to force Adam to pay more attention to her and the children.

Codependents will eventually detach themselves. They don't communicate, don't touch, don't feel, and don't trust. No wonder true intimacy escaped Adam completely. Adam's emotional development was arrested—frozen—when he was still a young man. It would be years before his development would pick up where it left off.

Adam found it hard to be himself around other people. Low self-esteem pushed him to constant efforts to be noticed, and he looked for anything outside himself to make himself feel better. This meant getting buried in school and work where achievement can be regularly and visibly recognized and rewarded. The need to be needed is compelling and compulsive. Codependents can become caretakers, a task in itself that can lead to utter and total exhaustion since the need to be needed never diminishes. When caretaking becomes compulsive, the codependent becomes a victim, feeling he has no choice and is helpless to break the cycle.

In part this was the allure of ministry for Adam. It provided an avenue for success in helping others that would be acknowledged as worthwhile. Yet it also resulted in collecting the needy and surrounding himself only with those who needed him emotionally or physically. Those who may not have "needed" him in this sense still had to relate to him on his terms—and those were usually very structured—and this helps explain why Adam had so few real friends.

Adam had trouble with boundaries, tended to be rigid, had difficulty adjusting to change, feared the transparency and vulnerability intimacy requires, felt guilty when asserting himself, and found himself in constant need of approval and recognition. By this time in his life, Adam could only "love" people he could pity and rescue.

Lack of trust, a constant need to control, poor communications, chronic anger: this was the Adam who sat across from me the day we first talked openly about his struggles. The harder he tried, the farther he drove others away and the more desperate, depressed, and unhealthy he became. Here is what we did to get Adam back on track physically, emotionally, and spiritually.

Adam knew I worked for an organization that provided outpatient counseling services and ran a small psychiatric hospital. He was at a point where he recognized the need to get help but didn't know what to do, and even if he did, he certainly lacked the physical and emotional energy to put it into action. I recommended the psychiatrist who provided the physical and admitted Adam to the hospital for a few days for evaluation both physically and mentally. This was when all the physical maladies were unmasked. An antidepressant was prescribed to help stabilize his mood, and Adam began a nutritional and exercise regimen along with counseling.

In time Adam recovered enough physically to be referred to a psychologist to begin dealing with underlying issues. His wife began participating in the counseling sessions as well.

Adam's temptation, because he was feeling better physically, was to get out of the program. Fortunately, he did not, but remained faithful to his weekly appointments and homework assignments. There were a lot of layers to peel back before Adam began to understand what needed to be unlearned and why.

Insight never cured anyone, but insight into a false belief can enable a person to make specific application to thinking and acting differently and building new and healthier physical and emotional habits. Adam is no different from many men whose attempts at self-rescue have ruined careers, marriages, and families. Adam also began to embrace a number of spiritual myths men tend to harbor that are obstacles to physical, emotional, and spiritual health.

First is the myth of the impossible example. We (men) can easily believe that Jesus is not quite just like us, even though the Word of God repeatedly emphasizes that truth. In part this is because our image of God is informed by our relationship with our earthly dads, and that is not always the best yardstick. In part this is because we really like it when we have an excuse, some logical (to our way of thinking) reason for excusing our behaviors. In part this is because an absolute standard—perfection—is out of reach, and we are less accountable in our own minds for achieving an unrealistic standard. We let ourselves off the hook.

This Adam is like the first Adam of the Bible, still trying to hide. Here is how it works: Jesus is the Son of God. He controlled nature, walked on water and through walls, healed the sick, and raised the dead. He has the power of the Almighty at his fingertips! Being born as an infant, growing up as an adolescent, and developing as a young man, he had all this power available to him. When Jesus was tempted, even though he was a man of flesh, this power as the Son of God enabled him to resist evil, make the correct decisions, and maintain his self-control. After all, Jesus is God; and you certainly cannot expect that kind of performance from me.

Hebrews 5:2 describes Jesus this way, "He can have compassion on those who are ignorant and going astray, since he himself is also subject to weakness." If Jesus was perfect and all-powerful, why is he described as subject to weakness? That certainly does not sound like perfection. Further in the same passage we find, "Though He was a Son, yet He learned obedience by the things which He suffered" (v. 8). Why would Jesus need to learn anything, particularly by suffering?

When the Scriptures tell us Jesus was a man, it means just that. He is a man in every way just as we are physically, emotionally, and spiritually. Jesus had available to him the same resources we do when it comes to dealing with temptation, making choices, and doing the right thing. Jesus did all this, and more, without sin. What a marvelous example for us! We can succeed! We can continue to grow in Christlikeness through weakness, learning obedience through the trials and tribulations of life. Jesus Christ purposefully gave up every advantage in order to experience life as we do and demonstrate the victory that can be ours.

Second is the myth of clairvoyant understanding. Under our skin we men really believe we are responsible to fix things, solve problems, make things right. It's in our genes. This presumes, of course, that we know what's wrong. Somehow we have this clairvoyance about what our problems are when this myth is applied personally. Now, the problem isn't in being a conquering/warrior/manly man kind of person. Part of that really is hardwired into the design God gave us. The problem is in the presumption that we can accurately self-diagnose what is wrong with us. Often when others think we may be reluctant to seek help because of a pride issue, the reason more accurately is because we really believe we know what the problem is.

"Who can understand his errors? Cleanse me from secret faults. Keep back Your servant also from presumptuous sins; Let them not have dominion over me. Then I shall be blameless, And I shall be innocent of great transgression" (Ps. 19:12–13). David, who had trouble seeing a problem with adultery and murder, was making the point here that our problems are not always obvious to us. Adam needed to look for solutions beyond his own opinions and understandings.

Third is the myth of the unchanging man. I am too old to change, I am what I am, you can't teach an old dog new tricks, I will always be this way, and other messages of denial characterize this myth.

In reality change is always possible. Even physically this is true. You have heard the sayings about how many weeks it takes to break a habit and how many weeks it then takes to build a habit. Though the estimates vary, they are based on a sound principle. New ways of thinking or acting build new neuronal pathways in the brain. Each new pathway takes about twenty-three days to form. Enough new neuronal pathways and you have a new habit. Now that is an oversimplification, but you get the idea: you can unlearn and you can learn new things.

Paul said in Ephesians 4:23 that we can be "renewed in the spirit of your mind." If our minds can potentially be reprogrammed physically and emotionally, why can't they be changed spiritually as well? Unlearning begins in the mind. Adam had much to unlearn.

Fourth is the myth of negative exposure. Men believe exposure is a bad thing. In fact, we work at hiding so thoroughly that not only do we hide our feelings from others; we actually can repress them and hide them from ourselves. Yet key to unlearning is exposing our poor strategies and motivations. Peter learned this the hard way. "Then he began to curse and swear, 'I do not know this Man of whom you speak!' A second time the rooster crowed. Then Peter called to mind the word that Jesus had said to him, 'Before the rooster crows twice, you will deny Me three times.' And when he thought about it, he wept" (Mark 14:71–72).

Exposure is painful and painfully necessary for us to have our true motivations exposed. We need to know victory is possible, that we don't have all the answers, that we can change, and that in order for that to occur we need to know our true motivations.

All of this "putting off" and "putting on," as Paul described unlearning and learning in Ephesians, is sometimes hard, dirty work. However, as my mentor used to say, if you don't face the pain now, you will be in pain the rest of your life.

Adam learned to love. His world has changed forever because he chose to face the pain knowing that healthy loves best.

Chapter Twenty

Where Do We Go from Here?

It would be easy to suggest reviewing each chapter for those things that made sense to you or pricked your heart regarding applications you could put into action right now. Only that really would not affect your character. My character has changed over the years not as a function of new knowledge or new skills, but from becoming a different person, from being and not from doing. God is interested in each of us becoming a different person.

I can successfully put into action all of the recommendations Paul listed in these few short verses we have been studying. I can work diligently at not doing the things he said we should put off because love doesn't act that way and I can work even harder at acting toward others in the ways he described we should love one another. All of that will not change who

I am underneath it all. I can't act my way into better character. I have to become a better person.

Isaiah carried this message to his countryman, "Therefore the Lord said: 'Inasmuch as these people draw near with their mouths and honor Me with their lips, but have removed their hearts far from Me'" (Isa. 29:13). God wanted their hearts, and He wants ours. That means any application we make must come from the heart and not from a need to act right or look good.

There is something we can work on, though, that enables us to respond to opportunities to change whenever they come along. Authenticity. The more authentic we are as men, the more receptive we become to opportunities to build character. To be authentic is to be real, genuine, true, undoubted, believable, valid, trustworthy, and credible. It is easier to understand how authenticity gives power and credibility to your character when you consider the alternatives: to be less than real, a counterfeit, false, doubtful, not believable, invalid, untrustworthy, or not credible.

Perhaps you have run into too-good-to-be-true people in your career. Very successful, they seem to land on their feet after every upset, always have a ready answer, and seem to be able to finesse their way to the top. Smooth talkers, there doesn't seem to be any reason to question their ability or credentials. They produce results, are well liked. Still there is just something that gives you a niggle. Something just isn't right.

Recently one of these smooth talkers was in the news. He landed a prestigious job as head coach for a major Midwestern university, having been recruited away from another well-known school. His track record as a coach was impressive.

The scam was up, however, when the university checked his background. He didn't have the master's degree he said he had and had a different undergraduate degree than stated on his application. His track record as a winning coach, going back several institutions, could not be verified; and his work record did not check out either. He was dismissed in disgrace.

How did he pass scrutiny for so long? Easy, he looked authentic, talked the right game, and no one bothered to check out his bona fides simply because he did look so good. This larger-than-life coach kept substituting until there was no real substance left in his life, and the whole story caved in on itself.

It may not be obvious at first, but we all take shortcuts when it comes to authenticity. "There is a path before each person that seems right, but it ends in death" (Prov. 16:25). Shortcuts always look good but are seldom as profitable as they appear.

Motive is the measure of authenticity. What motive might one have to be less than authentic? A need to look good? A desire to get ahead quickly? An opportunity to surpass the competition? Pressure to perform? Something to protect? Fear of exposure? Distaste for rejection? Allure of acceptance? Fear of failure? Approval of others? A bonus to qualify for? A promotion in the offing? I don't know about you, but all of these at one time or another have been a temptation for me.

Some would say that faking it is just as good as the real thing. After all, if perception is 100 percent of reality for most people, why not build on the perception. What does it matter if reality is different if faking it gets results for you and the company? One big problem: Sooner or later life is going to come along as it did for the head coach and demand that you live up to the perceptions you have created. Most men I talk to think they are authentic, believing the question has more to do with manhood than character. Here is a comparison of authentic and nonauthentic behaviors that may help illustrate the difference.

Skill/ Perspective	Authentic Behavior	Nonauthentic Behavior
Moral Authority	What you say is what you do.	What you say is not modeled in your behavior.
Alignment	You reproduce the organization's values in others.	You reproduce your personal values in others regardless of the organization's values.
Motivation	You create an environment that accomplishes the organization's goals.	You create an environment that accomplishes your personal goals regardless of what the organization's goals may be.
Learning	You are invested in the development of others.	You are not interested in the development of others.
Communication	Your communication engages others in dialogue.	Your communication inevitably centers on you.
Listening	You work to draw others out, especially when they have different views from your own.	You are constantly thinking about your next response while the other is talking.
Authority	Your authority is exercised in pursuit of the best outcome for all concerned.	Your authority is exercised for personal reasons, seeking to achieve something important to you alone.
Self-Management	You practice self-control.	You are prone to frequent outbursts.
Emotions	Shared appropriately with transparency.	Suppressed altogether or selectively used to manipulate the situation.

Skill/ Perspectives	Authentic Behavior	Nonauthentic Behavior
Choices	Focus on what is good or right.	Focus on your personal agenda regardless of what may be good or right.
Ethical Judgment	Based on an acceptable fixed standard.	Based on a relative frequently changing standard.
Arguing	Based on principle.	Based on ambition.
Dealing with Constraints	Viewed as process issues.	Viewed as personal obstacles.
Competence	Gets the job done, accepts responsibility when it doesn't happen.	Makes excuses, blames others.
Reconciliation	Apologizes with sincerity.	Rarely apologizes.
Failure	Deals with openly.	Rarely admits.
Serving	Known for being a servant.	Known for serving only when it increases personal stature with others.
Humility	Puts the interests of others or the organization first.	Puts self-interest first.
Flexibility	Sponsors appropriate change.	Resists appropriate change.
Ambition	Ambitious for others, for the cause.	Ambitious for self.
Authenticity	Known as a "real" person.	Is not known on a personal level at all, or is known as a self-seeking disingenuous person.

In one sense the behaviors identified as "not authentic" could be described as real because they do represent the person exhibiting these behaviors accurately, albeit negatively. "Authenticity" as discussed here has to do with being genuine in the sense of an altruistic standard. Measured against what gives you credibility and power as a person, *authentic* is a superlative, not a negative, and speaks to the real value of each attribute. Which person would you have confidence in, the one whose behaviors are more authentic or the one less authentic in his behaviors? Which one has more value to you personally? Which one would you look forward to spending time with?

When we gauge authenticity in others, we tend to use our own internal yardstick. That is, we view authenticity in others the same way we view it in ourselves. This may be unfair since genuine authenticity means different things for different people and in some part is a reflection of our enculturation and socialization. For example, different social paradigms are influenced by different cultural norms.

Those born before 1946 have a respectful view of authority. Baby boomers born between 1946 and 1964 tend to view authority with a love-hate relationship. They value freedom (their own) and control (of subordinates). Generation X, born between 1965 and 1976, are unimpressed by authority while Generation Y, born between 1977 and 1986, define authority in terms of teamwork and how the group exercises authority. Needless to say, each of these generations has a different perspective on authenticity.

The point is that we need to be careful that we do not label people as inauthentic simply because what constitutes being a real person for them may be different from what it is for us. The Veterans (pre-1946) will tend to view being a real person as someone who doesn't share a lot of his real feelings and doesn't require that of others either. Being real for them means maintaining an appropriate distance relationally. They may be authentic in the sense we are discussing in this chapter, but that will not be discovered by observation alone. You are going to have to engage them in conversation and draw them out.

Boomers will tend to be more confrontational and more ready to tell you what they are thinking—and want to know what you are thinking. For them hypocrisy is an issue. *Do you walk your talk?* is the measure of authenticity. Authenticity for Generation X is viewed in terms of self-reliance. In other words, *How self-actualized are you?* Generation Y is going to be more concerned with morality and what can they observe or learn about your character that may tell them how authentic you may be.

What is it that is so attractive about authentic people? Is it their gifts, talents, or success? No, it is the fact that authentic people do not hide their brokenness. This willingness to share weakness actually produces the strength authentic men bring to their character.

Authenticity begins with self-awareness. I once worked with an attorney who was not very self-aware and not very authentic. A good enough attorney, he was insensitive to the manner in which he always took center stage. Grant always turned conversations into a struggle over who was in control of the dialogue. If someone had a unique experience, Grant always had a better story to tell. If someone challenged his opinion, he or she was quickly marginalized. His approach to a problem was not only the right one; it was the only one in his mind. Control and preeminence were utmost and foremost in Grant's demeanor, discussion, and deportment. The guy had an ego that would not quit and seemed unwilling or unable to recognize the problem.

When this shortcoming was pointed out from time to time, he was responsive, quick to apologize and seek reconciliation. Ego would be reined in for a time until the same character flaw would emerge again, usually with efforts to insert himself into decisions or processes where his involvement was unwelcome or unneeded.

This singular character flaw compromised the very real contribution Grant could have made. The world had to revolve around Grant. He wanted to make a difference and was committed to change. Grant's problem was that he was attempting to address the symptoms and not the underlying cause. He was trying to act differently, not be different; and it eventually cost him a lucrative job. If you desire to be authentic, you have to be self-aware.

There was a time when my peers at work confronted me with a flaw I was not aware of at all. In my efforts to look good and get ahead, I had a tendency to exaggerate. As a result I gave the impression of having more influence on outcomes than I really did. This was embarrassing and humiliating. However, I swallowed my pride, took responsibility, asked forgiveness, and made an effort to understand the roots of my behaviors from their perspectives.

The outcome of those conversations started me on the road to greater authenticity. Years later, when my former boss was asked for a recommendation by an employer considering hiring me, he said, "If ever I have the chance to put together a corporate dream team, Jeff would be my first pick." Evidently that singular recommendation from a credible source made the difference among a number of equally or better qualified candidates, and I got the job. This is all the more important considering that my former boss was among those who were concerned enough to address this issue in my life.

I was committed to character change, not just suppressing symptomatic behavior. Working on authenticity left me receptive to the opportunity to take their feedback seriously and make a difference in my world. Authentic people are receptive.

That wasn't the first or last time I have had an opportunity to improve. My character, like yours, is a work in progress. What people want to know about you and me is whether or not we are dealing with what we know we need to deal with and are willing to admit we are a work in progress.

Disingenuous people do not get ahead for long. Imperfect people who respond to their flaws with genuine acknowledgement and compelling efforts to change at fundamental levels do get ahead. Why? Because people can trust you to deal appropriately with reality and not ignore it, excuse it, or blame it on others. Authenticity builds trust. Trust is foundational to lasting success.

Spiritual maturity is not possible without some degree of authenticity. Spiritual maturity brings with it an ability to recognize and deal with reality and an ability to adapt to changing circumstances and changing relationships in non-destructive ways.

Grant was not able to do that effectively. His perception of reality was one in which he held an inflated view of himself, and when circumstances changed, he often responded in immature ways.

Grant joined my team briefly during an intense business negotiating session. He was just supposed to observe but could not resist the temptation to interject his opinions. When it became clear he was literally taking over the meeting in a demanding and pugnacious manner, a break was called. In the corridor Grant was reminded that he was there just to observe. He agreed that he would keep his mouth shut and not interfere.

Well, that didn't last long. He got his attitude bent out of shape about something and jumped right in, making everyone on both sides of the issue unhappy, even angry. He used language that was unacceptable, cast insults around like they were labels, raised his voice to shout down others before they were even through speaking. Basically Grant was working hard to bully everyone into his way of thinking. As the team leader, I had to pull the plug.

Back in the corridor we had a discussion about strategy, ethics, where all this was going, what my role was, and what I thought he understood his role was. He became increasingly argumentative and belligerent. I finally told Grant his behavior was unacceptable, he was off the team, and he needed to leave right then.

To my surprise, Grant got all puffed up, pushed himself up against me, got in my face, and said, "You got a problem? Let's go! Right now! We'll settle this in the parking lot!"

I was flabbergasted! I told Grant we weren't in grade school anymore and to knock it off. Later when things had cooled down, I sought him out to make amends as necessary. He was certainly apologetic but, once again, totally unaware of how egregiously immature his conduct had been.

Grant was provided a number of opportunities to improve over the next few months. He received coaching (in the positive sense of the word), his job assignment was changed to eliminate the kinds of situations prone to trigger problem reactions, and he agreed to a performance improvement plan. A lot of time and money was invested in Grant in an effort to improve his effectiveness. At the end of the plan, Grant's attitude was that he was now healed.

Just saying you are healed does not make it so. You can't heal a wound by just saying so. "They have also healed the hurt of My people slightly, Saying, 'Peace, peace!' When there is no peace" (Jer. 6:14). God's people had this problem also—believing things were different just because they said so. I am grateful I wasn't around when he got canned. I can just imagine the eruption!

Grant had built his self-esteem on the wrong things and consequently was not genuine, authentic, or willing to consider that he wasn't either of these things. Lots of things go into creating healthy self-esteem, but sustaining self-esteem requires a solid foundation in being productive, solid relationships, and healthy recreation.

If your work is meaningful to you, if you experience an appropriate intimacy in your closest relationships, and if you are engaged regularly in activities that bring you joy just from the sheer pleasure of doing them, then you have a solid foundation that will nurture and support healthy self-esteem.

So where do we go from here? If we are working on authenticity, the applications will make themselves obvious. Self-awareness and healthy self-esteem are the tools that enable men to be authentic. Authentic men of character can change the world.

Chapter Twenty-One

---◆---

For Women Only

If you asked Adam what he was looking for in a mate, he probably would have told you a woman who is not neurotic and has a short list of what she wants in a man. Eve, on the other hand, probably would have said she was looking for a man who could engage her emotionally, gets a good paycheck, loves to hang out, and is in touch with her moods. Right from the start we are set up for problems because expectations are so different. Not only are men and women different from each other, men are different from one another as well.

The Broadmoor Hotel complex in Colorado Springs, Colorado, straddles a lake sitting at the foot of Pikes Peak. Every year geese fly in and make the lake a stopover on their journey to wherever they may be going in the seasonal migration. Nancy and I enjoyed walking around the lake, often just sitting for a while, and watching the geese. Some days the lake would be nearly filled with floating geese napping, nibbling, or neatly paddling to and fro.

It occurred to me one day that the geese in the lake did not follow a pattern or stay in formation like they do when flying. Each one floats pointing in a different direction doing different things but still hanging together.

I learned later that this behavior, everyone pointed in a different direction doing different things, actually is instinctual conduct designed to protect the geese. One of them is always looking in every direction. When danger comes, those that spot it first take action to wing away. Others pick up on the motion, and soon the whole flock is storming off the lake in a noisy flap of wings amid squawks of protest and alarm. In action the geese look all the same. At rest it is clear they are all very different individuals. That is true for men too.

It is easy, ladies, to think we are all the same; and the differences we share as men only compound the problems we experience due to the differences in gender. As important as understanding differences are, however, it is not differences that are the source of problems. Disrespect ultimately is at the root of problems, and not acknowledging a difference— treating us all the same—is a fundamental form of disrespect. A man would rather leave than live with disrespect.

It began a long time ago. And they heard the sound of the LORD God walking in the garden in the cool of the day, and Adam and his wife hid themselves from the presence of the LORD God among the trees of the garden. Then the LORD God called to Adam and said to him, "Where are you?" So he said, "I heard Your voice in the garden, and I was afraid because I was naked; and I hid myself." And He said, "Who told you that you

were naked? Have you eaten from the tree of which
I commanded you that you should not eat?" Then the
man said, "The woman whom You gave to be with me,
she gave me of the tree, and I ate." (Gen. 3:8–12)

Our instinctive response as men when confronted is to
run for the bushes. If hiding doesn't work, we go for strategy
number two: blame someone else. If that doesn't work, we can
turn on the avoidance radar: staying away because of work,
golf, or home improvement projects. We even have an attack
strategy, shouting, losing our tempers, attacking with a verbal
barrage impossible to refute or creating a fortress of emotional
and physical abuse we hide behind because we have made it
too painful for someone else to scale the walls. It is all just a
version of running for the bushes. We are so good at it that even
while hiding we can appear to be altogether, strong, wise, and
successful.

We like to hide. The key for men is to be coaxed out of
hiding. Respect does this more effectively than anything else
does. You see, we need to know that it is safe to be broken
around you. Everyone is broken, even the best of men. "For
we all stumble in many things. If anyone does not stumble in
word, he is a perfect man, able also to bridle the whole body"
(James 3:2). Here are some things that are not respectful of our
brokenness. (As a man I can learn from these stories as well.
They help inform me how others may respond to how I choose
to love them.)

Imagine how Eve felt when she heard Adam blame her.
Of course, she was hiding also, well aware of her role in all of
this; and she was quick to pass responsibility on to the serpent
herself. When we blame others it is all about number one. We
seldom think of how others, may feel about what we say. When
someone blames us, it makes us feel condemned. We may

even want to take responsibility, do the right thing, but it is a struggle when we are dealing with all the negative emotions blaming has produced. Our temptation is to stay hidden.

Unconditional love does not produce feelings of rejection like blame does—especially when we may know we really are guilty. "What shall we say then? Is there unrighteousness with God? Certainly not! For He says to Moses, 'I will have mercy on whomever I will have mercy, and I will have compassion on whomever I will have compassion.' So then it is not of him who wills, nor of him who runs, but of God who shows mercy" (Rom. 9:14–16). God's love is unconditional, and he does not base his acceptance of us upon our performance. Instead, we find mercy. I am not so perfect that Nancy does not at some point disapprove of something I may have said or done. However, I am so convinced of her acceptance that I find it easy, in fact I am often eager, to accept responsibility. She has coaxed me out of the bushes.

Though we learn little more about the dialogue between Adam and Eve once they are out of the garden, you can bet they had many opportunities to discuss their responses to God in that encounter. How tempting it must have been, as the days, weeks, months, and years went by, and Adam repeatedly passed off his responsibility to someone or something else for Eve to say, "There you go again! You are so wishy-washy! I know I can always depend on you to be Mr. Inconsistent!" God is not upset by our inconsistencies. "As a father pities his children, So the LORD pities those who fear Him. For He knows our frame; He remembers that we are dust. As for man, his days are like grass; as a flower of the field, so he flourishes" (Ps. 103:13–15). In the big picture God knows how frail we are and understands weakness. He does not punish us for our lack of perfection.

When Nancy wants to point out my irritating inconsistencies, she does not make flat statements. She asks questions, draws me out, and seeks to understand the context. In the process the inconsistencies that are frustrating her usually become obvious to me. No, it is not a matter of politically correct language or being supersensitive not to offend or anger. Nancy can be excruciatingly direct. She is simply trying to understand me and not demand that I understand her in the moment. Her lack of demandingness frees my heart to engage in self-examination rather than self-protection. She is coaxing me out of the bushes.

If I were Eve, I could easily be angry with Adam for blame shifting with me as the target. I can imagine her grumbling, "I am going to make you pay!" Now we don't know if that happened at all. Eve could have been a sweetie pie without ever having given a single thought to punishing Adam. But you get the point: some people believe retribution is a lifestyle.

God does not hold grudges. "He will not always strive with us, Nor will He keep His anger forever. He has not dealt with us according to our sins, Nor punished us according to our iniquities. For as the heavens are high above the earth, So great is His mercy toward those who fear Him; As far as the east is from the west, So far has He removed our transgressions from us" (Ps. 103:9–12). When you know someone just isn't going to let it go and beat you up about it to boot, you tend to stay away. Frankly, it's safer in the bushes.

Condemnation, demands to be perfect or at least consistent, and getting even are fundamentally destructive to relationships. More important, they are thinly veiled forms of disrespect that any man is going to rebel against at the core of his being even if he knows his own failings brought it on.

Why are they disrespectful? They do not allow us to be broken, and even God allows us to be broken. If I can't trust you with my brokenness, what can I trust you with?

Love that is patient and kind, that can change the world of your man forever, that is consistent day after day and never fails, recognizes and respects differences. Keep in mind that there are no guarantees. Even Jesus could not keep everyone encouraged and connected. "From that time many of His disciples went back and walked with Him no more" (John 6:66).

Some of his followers found it too difficult and chose an easier path. You will not be able to keep everyone out of the bushes by the change in your love for him. Here are some interesting insights about how men think that may help shift your expectations and make a difference in the life of someone you love.

Let's start with a simple illustration. How do men think about money? Men tend to look at money one of two ways. Money is either a tool or a possession. If money is a possession, there will never be enough. You always have to save against potential disaster, or there is the bigger house, better car, newer toys, and so on. The pursuit of money and things never comes to an end, and no matter how successful you are in getting money, there just never seems to be enough.

When money is a tool, it becomes a means to an end and not the end in itself. The savings account has a purpose; you choose not to live beyond your means. Forgoing the bigger house, newer car, and all those toys enables you to be charitable as well as become debt free. Men who treat money as a possession are compensating for something.

Now let's bump it up a little bit and talk about memory. Memory works differently for men as well. Nancy can remember a lot of little key memories that helped form her life:

a third-grade school yard fight, admonishment from a favorite aunt, encouragement from a favorite teacher—things that resonate in our minds for a lifetime. Men can recall these kinds of formative memories as well. It just takes work. My brain works differently from Nancy's.

Now bring it forward. Can you imagine Eve talking to Adam, "Dear, remember when we were talking to the Smiths about coming over and looking at their stone house when it was finished?" Adam's response is a simple, "Huh?"

This doesn't mean he is brain-dead or really doesn't want to go and is just playing dumb. Give Adam a little more information to dig the memory out of the back of his head. Where were you when the Smiths issued this invitation? What was the occasion that brought you together? How long ago did this take place?

Men tend to need more of a context than women do to pull memories off the shelf because we tend to compartmentalize more. Whereas for women staying connected is often a greater need than it is for men and where, what, and when memories tend to maintain those connections.

We also have the ability to put the mind in neutral. Sometimes we really are thinking about nothing. This makes it difficult for us to convince you we are not being evasive. Some time ago Nancy and I had a very emotional conversation about the children, especially the oldest. After quite a bit of soul-searching and brainstorming, we ended the conversation. Nothing was resolved yet, but we both recognized some things were just out of our hands; and, as discouraging as that might be, it was reality.

Some minutes later Nancy observed from the family room that I was wandering around in the kitchen, staring off into nowhere, randomly opening cupboards as if it was just something to do. She got up from her chair and came into the kitchen and put her arms around me and said, "I'm sorry you are discouraged. I know it is tough to know the right thing to do. What are you thinking about?"

I looked at her for a moment and said honestly, "Bacon." She looked at me for a moment and then burst out laughing. Nancy realized that this deep thought she believed our conversation had propelled me into was nothing more than my being hungry and wandering around the kitchen looking for something to eat. Sometimes we really are thinking about nothing important.

OK, we can look at some more complex social situations. Men are by design doers, achievers, makers, workers; and we want to accomplish something. This can give some the impression we are also fixers—everything from a bad debt to a broken heart. Asking men to fix something vicariously by dumping responsibility on them is like asking a doctor to cure cancer, transplant a brain, or remove a birth defect. The doctor may or may not have the knowledge, skills, and training to come through for you. Men can't really solve everything.

In a group of strangers, men will use idle conversation to provide distance and safety while they decide, Can I trust you? Do you like me? Do I like you? In the same situation women can go deep quickly because their greater need is not for safety but for connection. Men tend to communicate who they are in terms of what they have done (remember, we are doers).

So, at the Smiths' housewarming party, Adam is telling everyone about his stone house while standing around with the guys in their fig leaves. Eve overhears and thinks, *What a chump! We are here at the Smiths' to celebrate their new house, and all he and the other guys can do is brag about their own!* Though the conversation may seem braggadocios to Eve, it really is an inoffensive language to men. This is the way men connect.

We have taken a peek at what goes on inside a guy's head that may be different from what you may expect and why social interactions among men have a different content and tone to them than what you may enjoy with other women. Here is an insight regarding trust and respect from a man's perspective that reflects these differences.

Adam came to Eve one day with a real burden to apologize for blaming her in the garden that day long ago. He remembered the event well. It was a life-changing memory. Ever since leaving the garden, he had tried to make it up to Eve. Adam worked hard, but there just never seemed to be enough. What God said about toil was turning out to be true.

Adam's hard work was his way of making it right, making up to Eve, compensating for his embarrassment and inability just to come right out and take responsibility and apologize. On the few occasions he did try to talk to Eve, she seemed more interested in having him just fix things than really draw him out. Most of the time Eve tried to second-guess his thinking and often misunderstood what he was trying to say. They couldn't even agree on the specifics of what happened. They couldn't seem to connect on this issue, and Adam had come to the point of realizing a solution to this problem was beyond him. He just couldn't fix it.

Adam wants to confide the deepest secrets of his soul to Eve. Men will confide the deepest secrets of their soul to someone they trust. The fact that Adam was not or could not confide in Eve in this way signals a trust issue. Either Adam is not capable of trusting, or Eve is not capable of being trusted. Nothing communicates inward trust more effectively than outward respect. This is Eve's cue to respect her man.

Respect is crucial to a man. A man naturally responds to high expectations. However, we want to earn that respect. It is part of our design to conquer, win, do, achieve, and accomplish. When we sense someone significant in our lives has low expectations of us, does not respect us, it becomes permission for us to do nothing. How many men have you seen respond positively to women who do not respect them?

We go away—literally or emotionally—to a place or a relationship where we can find respect. We go back to the bushes. On the other hand, we can accept and survive an enormous amount of someone's displeasure if we know we are respected and that respect is reflected in the highest expectations for us. For Adam and Eve it was a process of learning to love the way Paul described in 1 Corinthians 13. The breakthrough comes when love rejoices in the truth, bears all things, believes all things, hopes all things, and endures all things.

Thank you, Nancy, for changing my world.

—◆—

Chapter Twenty-Two

The Great Commandment

The words of 1 Corinthians 13:4–8 didn't just drop off the end of the pen as the letter to the Corinthians was being written. They were not an afterthought, a way to fill up the space on the page, or simply what came to mind at the time. They were written with intention backed by centuries of exposition and thought-about love. Hebrew theologians and legal scholars had wrestled with the concept of love as God defines it from their earliest history as a budding nation. What Paul had to say came out of an important context.

Mark 12:28–34 captures the Great Commandment for us:

> Then one of the scribes came, and having heard them reasoning together, perceiving that He had answered them well, asked Him, "Which is the first

commandment of all?" Jesus answered him, "The first of all the commandments is: 'Hear, O Israel, the LORD our God, the LORD is one. And you shall love the LORD your God with all your heart, with all your soul, with all your mind, and with all your strength.' This is the first commandment. And the second, like it, is this: 'You shall love your neighbor as yourself.' There is no other commandment greater than these." So the scribe said to Him, "Well said, Teacher. You have spoken the truth, for there is one God, and there is no other but He. And to love Him with all the heart, with all the understanding, with all the soul, and with all the strength, and to love one's neighbor as oneself, is more than all the whole burnt offerings and sacrifices." Now when Jesus saw that he answered wisely, He said to him, "You are not far from the kingdom of God." But after that no one dared question Him.

This response of Jesus to a question about what is the most important law of all the laws to follow connects love of God with loving your neighbor as one great statement about love. This is where the idea of the Great Commandment comes from. However, these are really two separate ideas in the Law. The first, loving God, comes from Deuteronomy 6:5, "You shall love the LORD your God with all your heart, with all your soul, and with all your strength." The idea of loving your neighbor comes from Leviticus 19:18, "You shall not take vengeance, nor bear any grudge against the children of your people, but you shall love your neighbor as yourself: I am the LORD."

These two ideas had been formed into a couplet in Jewish literature and teaching long before the time of Christ and had found their way together to the top of the list of what people understood God expects of us. If we can satisfy the requirements of the Great Commandment, we will also have fulfilled everything else God requires of us. No wonder it is the Great Commandment!

In a similar circumstance a lawyer attempted to embarrass Jesus in front of his followers as they gathered together to debrief the on-the-job training just completed. The question this time had to do with eternal life; and the answer is strikingly similar, knowing that the Jews looked to the Law for the answer to this question as well.

> And behold, a certain lawyer stood up and tested Him, saying, "Teacher, what shall I do to inherit eternal life?" He said to him, "What is written in the law? What is your reading of it?" So he answered and said, "You shall love the LORD your God with all your heart, with all your soul, with all your strength, and with all your mind," and "your neighbor as yourself." And He said to him, "You have answered rightly; do this and you will live." But he, wanting to justify himself, said to Jesus, "And who is my neighbor?" (Luke 10:25–29)

Of course, Jesus went on at this point to illustrate whom the neighbor is with the story of the good Samaritan—pointing out that your neighbor is anyone in need.

Love and its connection to the law, eternal life, and what God expects of mankind was not some obscure, obtuse subject. It was an idea that had been studied, debated, rehearsed, pondered, and written about for centuries. It was one of the first topics those that opposed Jesus sought to trip him up on, believing a carpenter's son would be no match for their scholarship. It wasn't a fuzzy subject to consider like it has become in modern times. Our love for God and our love for our neighbor was spoken about with clarity and understanding. Paul would have studied this subject thoroughly, but we will learn more about that in just a moment.

Jesus also provided a unique perspective on love for his followers. "A new commandment I give to you, that you love one another; as I have loved you, that you also love one another. By this all will know that you are My disciples, if you have love for one another" (John 13:34–35). It would seem on the face of it that Jesus was adding something to the Law. That is not the case. "New" here does not refer to chronology as in the sense of something brand-new as compared to something older. When we look at something in a different way, a way we may be unaccustomed to looking at it, it will appear new to us. That is the idea here. The commandment, as we have seen, is not new. In fact, it is a very old requirement. What Jesus was asking the disciples to do was to look at love in a new way, a way different from how they had considered love in the past.

Something about the quality of love was to be different for them. Jesus had modeled this difference for them over their months and years together: Helping others when it was not convenient, giving when it hurt, putting the interests of others before their own, forgiving others when they hurt them, refusing to complain and whine about the things in life they couldn't control, and by loving their neighbor the way Paul talked about it. This kind of sacrificial love that Jesus demonstrated for his disciples was different in form and substance from the love they had seen witnessed in the world around them. Paul captured the essence of his own heart regarding the newness of this commandment in his letter to the Galatians, "For all the law is fulfilled in one word, even in this: 'You shall love your neighbor as yourself'" (Gal. 5:14). Sacrificial love extended to anyone in need whether they deserved it or not. That might even be considered "new" these days as well.

As a Pharisee, Paul would have been well versed in the cultural and historical meaning of what was to become labeled the Great Commandment. His personal history lends even greater understanding of his focus on love in his letter to the Corinthians at a time when the church in Corinth was experiencing serious divisions over their conduct toward one another in everyday life.

Paul was born an Israelite in Tarsus of Cilicia, a Roman province. He would have been about two years younger than Jesus and would have been perhaps six or seven when Judea became a Roman imperial province. His father was a Pharisee of the tribe of Benjamin and a Roman citizen. Tarsus sat on the banks of the river Cydnus and was a major center of commerce both by water and by land. Tarsus was also a famous university city, even more famous at the time than Athens or Alexandria. Paul grew up in a wealthy aristocratic family, used to the privileges of a high social standing.

Growing up, Paul would have learned a trade before embarking on his professional career. This is how he became a tent maker. Probably around age thirteen Paul was sent to Jerusalem to study under Gamaliel, one of the leading Jewish legal scholars of the era. As a student at the Jewish School of Sacred Learning, Paul was being groomed to join the ruling elite of the nation. At some point after graduation, he returned to Tarsus.

However, he appears in Scripture back in Jerusalem soon after the death of Christ. Some believe it is possible he actually was in Jerusalem earlier and may have seen Jesus and thus was able to recognize him when he appeared to Paul in a vision on the road to Damascus. Others believe, understanding the words of Acts 9:5, "Who are You, Lord?" not so much as a question of confirmation but one of genuine inquiry, that Paul did not know who was appearing before him. In any event this young leader made it his business to stamp out the sect of followers of this so-called Messiah.

Paul would have been around thirty or thirty-one at the time of Christ's crucifixion. At the age of thirty, Paul would have been considered ready to enter into his professional career. His first big opportunity to accomplish something noteworthy in his career would have been this crusade to wipe out the Christians. He was very good at what he did, throwing people into jail, excommunicating them from the community, and meting out punishment up to and including death. Paul was responsible for the deaths of more than just a few believers. At some point it is understood that he became a member of the Sanhedrin, the ruling body in Israel.

As a Roman citizen he would have enjoyed special privilege in Roman-occupied Jerusalem; and as a highly educated Pharisee from the right family and tribe, he would have been in the upper crust of Jewish society. He was in a position where his word on something would have been the final word—legally, theologically, and spiritually. It would be interesting to compare his thoughts about love in those early days with those he would pen years later after his conversion.

Though we cannot do that, we can see the influence on his thinking as he began to grow in his new faith. Ananias took him briefly under his wing before Paul left for a long period of time. Paul spent a lot of time rethinking all that had been drilled into his head for thirty years, sorting it out, making the connections he had missed along the way—something we all need to do. When he resurfaced in Scripture, Barnabas took him under his wing. We know later that he spent time with the apostles, mentioning specifically Peter and James. Matthew cited the Great Commandment in his Gospel account as did Mark and Luke.

Can you imagine Paul discussing loving God and loving others with these men in the context of Jesus' "new" commandment? Historical tradition and Scripture make it clear that Luke, of all of them, seemed to hang out with Paul the most as time went by. No wonder Paul summarized his new understanding with, "You shall love your neighbor as yourself." He would take this message to most of the known world at the time.

Paul now knew the power of a loving man. It is a power that can change a life, change a family, change a neighborhood, change a city, change a nation, and change a world. In fact, it has done just that. In the few short words of 1 Corinthians 13:4–8, Paul unleashed years of careful thought shaped by experience, describing how this power is unleashed in our lives. If we can be men who love this way, there is no need for anything else.

The Great Commandment—all that God requires of us— boils down to these few simple action steps, "Love is patient and kind." This is the power of a loving man. With this power the heart is set free, and there is nothing we cannot accomplish to the glory of God. For centuries the answers to the questions: What does it mean to love God? and, What does it mean to love your neighbor? had been sought by those earnestly desiring to know how to apply what had been laid down in Deuteronomy 6:5 and Leviticus 19:18. Paul, in simple words expressed his hard-won understanding:

> Love suffers long and is kind; love does not envy; love does not parade itself, is not puffed up; does not behave rudely, does not seek its own, is not provoked, thinks no evil; does not rejoice in iniquity, but rejoices in the truth; bears all things, believes all things, hopes all things, endures all things. Love never fails.